Bloom's
GUIDES

Elie Wiesel's
Night

The Adventures of
  Huckleberry Finn
All the Pretty Horses
Animal Farm
The Autobiography of Malcolm X
The Awakening
The Bell Jar
Beloved
Beowulf
Brave New World
The Canterbury Tales
Catch-22
The Catcher in the Rye
The Chosen
The Crucible
Cry, the Beloved Country
Death of a Salesman
Fahrenheit 451
Frankenstein
The Glass Menagerie
The Grapes of Wrath
Great Expectations
The Great Gatsby
Hamlet
The Handmaid's Tale
Heart of Darkness
The House on Mango Street
I Know Why the Caged Bird Sings
The Iliad
Invisible Man
Jane Eyre

The Kite Runner
Lord of the Flies
Macbeth
Maggie: A Girl of the Streets
The Member of the Wedding
The Metamorphosis
Native Son
Night
1984
The Odyssey
Oedipus Rex
Of Mice and Men
One Hundred Years of Solitude
Pride and Prejudice
Ragtime
A Raisin in the Sun
The Red Badge of Courage
Romeo and Juliet
The Scarlet Letter
A Separate Peace
Slaughterhouse-Five
Snow Falling on Cedars
The Stranger
A Streetcar Named Desire
The Sun Also Rises
A Tale of Two Cities
The Things They Carried
To Kill a Mockingbird
Uncle Tom's Cabin
The Waste Land
Wuthering Heights

Bloom's
GUIDES

Elie Wiesel's
Night

Edited & with an Introduction
by Harold Bloom

BLOOM'S
LITERARY CRITICISM
An imprint of Infobase Publishing

Bloom's Guides: Night

Copyright © 2009 by Infobase Publishing

Introduction © 2009 by Harold Bloom

Bloom's Literary Criticism
An imprint of Infobase Publishing
132 West 31st Street
New York, NY 10001

Library of Congress Cataloging-in-Publication Data
Elie Wiesel's Night / [edited] by Harold Bloom.
   p. cm. — (Bloom's guides)
 Includes bibliographical references and index.
 ISBN 978-1-60413-198-7
 1. Wiesel, Elie, 1928– Nuit. 2. Authors, French—Biography—History and criticism. 3. Holocaust, Jewish (1939–1945), in literature. 4. Judaism and literature—France. I. Bloom, Harold.
 PQ2683.I32N8534 2009
 940.53'18071—dc22
                              2008037808

Bloom's Literary Criticism books are available at special discounts when purchased in bulk quantities for businesses, associations, institutions, or sales promotions. Please call our Special Sales Department in New York at (212) 967-8800 or (800) 322-8755.

You can find Bloom's Literary Criticism on the World Wide Web at
http://www.chelseahouse.com

Contributing Editor: Neil Heims
Cover design by Takeshi Takahashi
Printed in the United States of America
Bang EJB 10 9 8 7 6 5 4 3 2
This book is printed on acid-free paper.

Contents

Introduction

HAROLD BLOOM

Rather than comment directly upon Elie Wiesel's *Night*, which is the subject of all the essays in this volume, I will address myself to the larger question of Holocaust literature. My starting point will be Geoffrey Hartman's poignant and brilliant *The Longest Shadow: In the Aftermath of the Holocaust* (1996). Trauma, primary and secondary, respectively that of survivor or of audience, is at the center of Hartman's insights:

> I am hardly the first to worry about the increasing prevalence of psychic numbing accompanied by fascination, and which is usually the consequence of *primary* trauma. It would be ironic and sad if all that education could achieve were to transmit a trauma to later generations in secondary form. In this fifth decade after the collapse of the National Socialist regime, the disaster still has not run its course. No closure is in sight: the contradictory imperatives of remembering and forgetting are no less strong than before.

But that leads to the question of artistic representation: can you, should you, try to transmute the Holocaust into literature? Hartman defends the possibility of this transmutation against the Frankfurt Jewish philosopher, Theodor Adorno:

> After the Holocaust there is a spiritual hunt to de-aestheticize everything—politics and culture as well as art. As Adorno phrased in his harshest and most famous statement, it is a sign of the barbaric (that is, of lack of culture) to write poetry after Auschwitz. He refused the arts a role even in mourning the destruction, because they might stylize it too much, or "make unthinkable fate appear to have some meaning." Yet art creates

an unreality effect in a way that is *not* alienating or desensitizing. At best, it also provides something of a safe-house for emotion and empathy. The tears we shed, like those of Aeneas when he sees the destruction of Troy depicted on the walls of Carthage, are an acknowledgment and not an exploitation of the past.

To acknowledge without exploiting is a difficult burden: are any of us strong enough for that? Hartman crucially goes on to consider a great poet, Paul Celan, Romanian-Jewish by birth, who wrote in a purified German. Celan's parents were murdered in the Holocaust; the poet himself survived a labor camp, but killed himself in Paris, at the age of fifty. His art was one of reticence, stripping words of their images. Hartman again is precise and eloquent upon the effect:

> Trauma is given a form and disappears into the stammer we call poetry, into a fissure between speech on the page, seemingly so absolute, and an invisible writing that may not be retrievable. This is, in truth, a disaster notation.

Paul Celan was a great (and very difficult) literary artist. Elie Wiesel is an eminent Witness, but hardly a canonical writer of narrative. Yet only a moral idiot would react to Wiesel's *Night* by refusing the burden of secondary trauma. A purely aesthetic reaction to *Night* is impossible, and not to be urged upon anyone. There remains what I find most problematical for Wiesel's reader: How to find the strength to acknowledge *Night* without exploiting it?

Biographical Sketch

Elie Wiesel was born in the village of Sighet, in Transylvania, on September 20, 1928. Under Romanian control during most of Wiesel's youth, governance was transferred to Hungary in 1940. On May 16, 1944, deportation of the Jews of Sighet to the Nazi death camp Auschwitz in Poland began. Wiesel, his father, mother, and three sisters were sent there. His mother and younger sister were immediately killed. Wiesel and his father remained together in Auschwitz in its slave-labor section, Buna, throughout their incarceration. His father died of dysentery in Buchenwald approximately two months before the arrival of American armed forces and the liberation of the camp. After the liberation, unable to secure permission to settle in Palestine and not wishing to go back to Sighet, which was then occupied by troops of the Soviet Army, Wiesel was placed in an orphanage in France.

Until the disruption of his life by the Nazis, Wiesel had led a typical, middle-class life. His family was loving, cultured, prosperous, close-knit, well regarded in the community, and Orthodox. His father, Shlomo, was a grocer and one of the village elders, a leader in the Jewish community. He encouraged his son to study modern Hebrew—the Jews in Sighet spoke Yiddish—science, and Freudian psychology. Wiesel's mother, Sarah, was the daughter of a farmer and Hasid, a follower of a branch of mystical, Orthodox Judaism. She encouraged her son's study of Torah, the Hebrew scriptures; the Talmud, the compendium of Jewish law; and Kabbalah, the mystical Jewish study of the divine particularly in its aspect as an indwelling force. Young Elie was a devout and scholarly boy with a passionate attachment to Judaism and a fiery belief in and deep devotion to God.

Sixteen years old at the time of his arrival in France, Wiesel was placed in an orphanage and was reunited with his two elder sisters, Hilda and Bea, who had also survived the concentration camps. In 1948, Wiesel began living in Paris and registered at the Sorbonne where he studied literature, philosophy, and psychology. To earn money, he taught Hebrew. At this time, too, he began a career in journalism, writing for the French-Jewish paper, *L'Arche*, and for *Yediot Ahronot*, the newspaper of the Irgun, a Jewish group in Palestine dedicated to the creation of a Zionist state there. He came in contact with Irgun when he was on a newspaper assignment in Tel Aviv.

It was in his role as a journalist in 1954 or 1955 (the exact date is uncertain) that Wiesel met the French Catholic writer and winner of the 1952 Nobel Prize in literature, François Mauriac. During the course of the interview, Wiesel became upset by Mauriac's repeated references to the suffering inherent in the crucifixion and related some of the sufferings he had both witnessed and experienced in Auschwitz. In response, Mauriac wept at Wiesel's revelations and encouraged him to write about what he had undergone, something Wiesel had been unable to do despite his career as a journalist. When Wiesel began to relive his time in Auschwitz in writing, he produced a book of nearly eight hundred pages, written in Yiddish, published in Argentina by a Yiddish publishing house, and called *Un di velt hot geshvign (And the World Remained Silent)*. While in New York, in 1956, covering the United Nations for a French newspaper, Wiesel was hit by a car and suffered serious injury that required a ten-hour operation and an extended hospital stay. Unable to return to France because of his injuries and unable to renew the French visa on which he traveled as a stateless person, Wiesel applied for U.S. citizenship. He also set to work on transforming *Un di velt hot geshvign*. He cut the book down to a little more than one hundred pages and rewrote it in French. *La Nuit* was published in 1958, and its English translation appeared two years later.

Not an immediate popular success, nevertheless, in the course of a few years, *Night* became viewed as the main account of the Holocaust and Wiesel became, in his person, the foremost voice of the experience of the Holocaust. From 1972 to 1976, Wiesel served as a Distinguished Professor of Judaic Studies at the City University of New York. In 1978, he was appointed Andrew Mellon Professor of the Humanities at Boston University. In 1982, Wiesel became the first Henry Luce Visiting Scholar in Humanities and Social Thought at Yale University. In 1978, then U.S. president Jimmy Carter appointed Wiesel to head the U.S. Holocaust Memorial Council, which he did until 1986. In 1985, when Ronald Reagan, president at the time, awarded Wiesel the Congressional Gold Medal, Wiesel implored the president not to make a planned ceremonial visit to a cemetery in Bitburg, Germany, where SS men were buried, saying the president's place was with the victims of the SS. Reagan, nevertheless, made the visit. In 1986, Wiesel was awarded the Nobel Peace Prize. From 1997 to 1999, he was Ingeborg Rennert Visiting Professor of Judaic Studies at Barnard College.

In 2002, Wiesel returned, for the first time since the deportation, to Sighet where memorial status was conferred on the house in which he was born. He has been the recipient of numerous awards, has chaired many committees studying aspects of the Holocaust, and has been a notable voice in defense of many groups of oppressed people. His ardent support for Israel, however, has caused some to regret what they see as his inability to weigh the suffering of Palestinians in the conflict between Israel and Palestine.

Wiesel has also consistently been the target of Holocaust deniers, people who claim the Nazi program of Jewish extermination is a historical lie and that the Holocaust never happened. In 2007, he was attacked in an elevator in a hotel in San Francisco after addressing a conference there. Dragged from the elevator by a young man who intended to take him back to his room and make him confess that *Night* was a compendium of lies, Wiesel called for help and was rescued.

Wiesel married Marion Erster Rose in 1969. She was born in Austria and also survived incarceration in Nazi camps. She has served as translator for nearly all the books Wiesel wrote in French. They have a son, Shlomo Elisha Wiesel, named after Wiesel's father.

The Story Behind the Story

Night was written in part because Elie Wiesel, during an interview for a newspaper article he was writing, chaffed at Nobel Prize–winning French Catholic writer François Mauriac's repeated references to the crucified Christ's sufferings and responded by recounting some of the agonies he experienced and witnessed at Auschwitz. To his credit, Mauriac did not counter Wiesel's outburst and attempt to explain what Christ's passion signified to him and its applicability to Jewish suffering. Rather, he wept with Wiesel and encouraged him to write about what he had gone through.

Wiesel had already drawn up an outline for such an account in April 1945, following his liberation from Buchenwald, when he was hospitalized with food poisoning and on the brink of death. Wiesel had determinedly held back from writing such a book until Mauriac's encouragement. Then, after his encounter with Mauriac, on a trip to Argentina from France, Wiesel wrote *Un di velt hot geshvign (And the World Remained Silent)* a work of nearly eight hundred pages written in Yiddish. The book was produced by a Yiddish publishing house in Argentina in 1956. Its release garnered little attention.

In New York, covering the United Nations for a French newspaper later that year, Wiesel was seriously injured when he was hit by a car. During his recuperation he transformed *Un di velt hot geshvign*, 245 pages in its final published form, into a shortened account of a little more than one hundred pages and written in French. He called it *La Nuit (Night)*. *La Nuit* was not only shorter than *Un di velt* it was also more temperate in tone. While *La Nuit* begins anecdotally with a description of Moishe the Beadle, *Un di velt* begins with an angry parody of the opening of the book of Genesis:

> In the beginning was belief, foolish belief, and faith, empty faith, and illusion, the terrible illusion. . . . We believed in God, had faith in man, and lived with the illusion that in each one of us is a holy spark from the fire

of the shekinah, that each one carried in his eyes and in his soul the sign of God. This was the source—if not the cause—of all our misfortune.

Written in Yiddish, *Un di velt* was an angry book of purgation for Wiesel and, considering those who were able to read Yiddish at the time, for other Jews. In French and then in English, it became something else, the testimony of the witness presenting the Jewish plight to the non-Jewish world.

With Mauriac's help and after many rejections, *La Nuit* was published in France in 1958. Two years later, again after many rejections, often by publishers moved by the horror of the book but anxious about its marketability, it appeared in the United States in an English translation as *Night*. Despite positive reviews by such important critics as Alfred Kazin, *Night* drew little interest and sold poorly. Then the trial of Nazi war criminal Adolph Eichmann in Jerusalem in 1961 put the Holocaust on the front pages of world newspapers and the market for books like *Night* exploded. Because of its depiction of what it was like to be in Auschwitz and because of the theological importance of Wiesel's argument with God over God's puzzling and apparent indifference to man's fate, the book became iconic, one of the major Jewish texts of the Holocaust. Nearly fifty years later, when the influential television personality Oprah Winfrey recommended *Night* on her daytime television show, Wiesel's book returned to the best-seller lists and sold approximately three million copies in a period of eighty weeks, bringing the total sales of the book since it publication to more than ten million copies.

At the core of *Night* is the Nazi German campaign to exterminate Jews. The machinery of that project was a massive and complex engine of deportations, transportations, incarcerations, and exterminations carried out with both sadistic brutality and determination and an industrial precision that had never before been realized and whose organizational efficiency added an impenetrable cold-bloodedness to its horror. Wiesel and his family were among the millions caught up in that machinery.

After Germany's defeat in World War I and the fall of the government of the kaiser, and in part because of the punishing conditions of the Treaty of Versailles, the peace agreement that ended the war, the nation experienced a period of political and economic chaos that was brought to an end by the election of Adolph Hitler as chancellor in March 1933. Hitler imposed an iron, dictatorial rule on Germany, which he consolidated a little more than a year later in July 1934 with the massacre, called the Night of the Long Knives, of possible rivals for power within the Nazi Party.

One of the cornerstones of Hitler's program was an uncompromising vilification of Jews. His policy of anti-Semitism was never veiled; he had proclaimed it openly in *Mein Kampf (My Battle)*, the book he wrote in 1925 while briefly incarcerated in a German jail for having led an unsuccessful coup against the government, in November 1923, called the Beer Hall Putsch. Soon after Hitler's ascent to power, the German campaign against Jews began in earnest, in April 1933, with a boycott against Jewish businesses. Soon Jews were banned from professional positions. In 1935, the Nuremburg Laws were enacted. They were a series of statutes forbidding marriage or sexual relations between non-Jewish and Jewish Germans, stripping Jews of German citizenship, and declaring the Nazi party's swastika banner to be the flag of the nation. In 1940, the Nazis released, *Die Ewige Jude (The Eternal Jew)*, a profoundly anti-Semitic propaganda film in which Jews were defined not as human beings but as vermin by the juxtaposition of images of Jews and rats. In 1944, German troops entered Wiesel's Romanian village, Sighet.

Night is a memoir of the Jewish catastrophe written from the point of view of a man who has survived imprisonment in the death and slave labor camps. It is his anatomy of the events as wrought on the body and psyche of a boy of fifteen. It is an account of the initial denial and incomprehension of those Jews who did not take Hitler's threats seriously. It is a dumbfounded reproach to the rest of the world for letting the Holocaust and the related atrocities committed by the Germans occur. It is also a testimony to the absence of God, a lamentation whose theme is God's betrayal not only of Jews but of any responsibility in promoting justice and righteousness in the world. And it is a desperate prayer for a humane world in which people may act in the awareness and recognition of each other's humanity, for Wiesel shows that in Auschwitz the barbarous brutality only served to separate and alienate the prisoners forcing many to place their individual survival above all other concerns.

Night then is a book that allows its author to confront the past every time it is read and brings a new reader to that period of horror and depravity Wiesel and the others endured. The book is Wiesel's means of confronting, each time it is read, the men he could not confront then, the Nazis who brought torment to his life. As much as it is a book of witness, *Night* is a book of revolt, the voice of rebellion the author could not express at the time of his imprisonment, not a revolt against God but against the human brutality to which he had once been forced to submit. It is the reverberating echo of the cry he could not utter, all the louder now because it was silenced then.

Night is the book Wiesel wrote in order "to give some meaning to my survival." Writing this seminal work in the literature of the Holocaust was an act of purgation by a man who as a teenager was stuffed into a cattle car and sent on "a last voyage towards the unknown," who discovered "a demented and glacial universe where to be inhuman was human, where disciplined, educated men in uniform came to kill, and innocent children and weary old men came to die." It is a book where once more the astonishing horror confronts the author anew when he recalls "incredibly, the vanishing of a beautiful, well-behaved little Jewish girl with golden hair and a sad smile, murdered with her mother the very night of their arrival" (p. ix).

List of Characters

Alphonse is a Jewish group leader in Buna who champions his charges and gets them extra soup when he can.

Moishe Chaim Berkowitz is one of Eliezer's friends in Sighet who returns from a visit to Budapest and reports that Jews there are living in fear and terror. His report causes only brief anxiety in the Jewish community of Sighet.

Akiba Drumer is a religious, even mystical boy who knows many Hasidic melodies that he and Eliezer sing. Because of his incarceration, he loses his faith in God and his will to live and is picked for extermination at a "selection."

Rabbi Eliahu approaches Eliezer during the evacuation asking if he has seen his son, who he has lost. Eliezer answers that he has not. Once Rabbi Eliahu has gone, though, Eliezer recalls that he had seen Rabbi Eliahu's son who was well aware his father had fallen to the back of the group. Eliezer wonders if his son had not deliberately abandoned his father in order to focus all his energy on saving himself. Eliezer prays that he may never do what he attributes to Rabbi Eliahu's son, suggesting he fears that he may.

Franek, formerly a student in Warsaw, was the leader of the labor *Kommando* to which Eliezer was assigned in Buna. He torments Eliezer's father until the boy agrees to give him the gold crown on one of his teeth.

The **French woman in Buna** is a quiet young woman who works beside Eliezer but never speaks. Everyone is under the impression that she does not speak German. After he is severely beaten, she comforts him and, in German, encourages him to focus on the future. Years later, he meets her in the Paris Métro. They go to a café where she tells him that she, too, is Jewish but managed to survive by making the Nazis think she was not.

16

Miklos Horthy served as regent of Hungary after World War I and throughout World War II. When he is forced to appoint a fascist government, Wiesel notes, the Jews of Sighet were not unduly alarmed, although they should have been.

Idek is a *kapo* who has occasional violent tantrums. On one such occasion, he brutally beats Elizer.

Juliek is a Polish Jew in Buna and a violinist.

Mrs. Kahn, one of the Wiesels' neighbors in Sighet, is surprised at the friendliness of the occupying German troops. A German officer billeted in her house, she happily tells her neighbors, even presented her with a box of chocolates.

Béla Katz is one of the first people Eliezer and his father meet in Auschwitz. He is from Sighet, too, the son of a merchant in the town. Because of his strength, he was put to work in the crematoria and "had been forced to place his . . . father's body into the furnace."

Meir Katz, unrelated to Béla, is an inmate, a friend of Elie's father. His son was killed in Auschwitz during the first selection. Although a big and strong man, Meir Katz loses all vitality and dies in despair in the last convoy when the prisoners are evacuated from Buna and sent to Buchenwald.

Louis is a well-known Dutch violinist incarcerated in Buna.

Maria, not a Jew, worked as a maid for the Wiesels. When they are moved to the small ghetto in preparation for being transported, she offers to shelter them in her village but Elie's father refuses her offer.

Joseph Mengele, a doctor, was in charge of the "selection," choosing Jews for extermination, at Auschwitz.

Moishe the Beadle is an important figure in Eliezer's early life before the Jews of Sighet are transported to the death camps. He lives in poverty, takes care of the synagogue, keeps to himself, is cheerful, and is liked by the community. He notices Eliezer's piety, questions him about his religious beliefs, and begins a study of the Kabbalah with him when the boy expresses an interest. Moishe is deported before the other Jews of Sighet because he is not a native of the town. He manages to escape death at the hands of the Nazis and returns to Sighet to warn the Jews of the ongoing genocide that the Nazis are carrying out against Jews, but all refuse to heed his words, and his once cheerful disposition gives way to gloom.

The **Dutch** *oberkapo* and his *pipel*, or serving boy, are both loved by the other inmates. They are part of the resistance in the camp. Weapons are found hidden among their belongings. Both are tortured but reveal nothing. Later they are killed, the boy in a public hanging.

An elegant **Parisian lady** whom Wiesel encounters years after his liberation throws coins from the deck of a passenger liner to boys in the water, who fight with each other to retrieve the coins. She proudly tells Wiesel she likes to give charity when he asks her to stop, for it reminds him of how the Germans threw crumbs into a cattle car of starving Jews and enjoyed watching them struggle with each other for the crumbs.

A patient in the infirmary in the bed next to Eliezer tells him that he should not stay in the hospital too long, because the risk of selection there is even greater than in the rest of Buna.

A young Pole was in charge of a block that Wiesel and his father were assigned to in Auschwitz. Unlike everyone else in a position of authority, he is a kind person who addresses the prisoners with "human words" and as if he is one of them.

The chief rabbi of Sighet appears in the street for deportation, hunched over with a bundle on his back, his beard shaved off.

Mrs. Schächter is in the same cattle car with Eliezer when the Jews of Sighet are being transported to Auschwitz. She remarks throughout the journey that she sees fire, so disconcerting the others pressed into the cattle car that they pummel and bind her.

Stein is a prisoner in Auschwitz who finds Elie and his father. He introduces himself as the huband of Elie's mother's niece Reizel. When he asks if they had heard anything of Reizel before they were imprisoned, in order to keep up his spirit, Elie lies, telling him she sent letters to his mother and she and the children are well. After he learns the truth the following week from a newly arrived transport, Stein grows despondent and dies.

Tibi and **Yossi** are brothers, Zionists, and friends of Eliezer in Buna. Together they talk of the future and of going to Palestine once they are liberated. They go through a selection together.

Bea Wiesel is one of Elie's two elder sisters, only mentioned in passing. Though she survives the camps and is reunited with her brother after liberation, she does not figure in his narrative.

Eliezer Wiesel is the young Elie Wiesel, the narrator of *Night*. As a boy in Sighet he is devout, weeps when he prays, and studies Kabbalah with Moishe the Beadle. When the Jews are transported, he is taken to the Nazi death camp, Auschwitz, with his family and the rest of the Jews of Sighet. There he is separated from his mother and sisters. With his father, he avoids cremation, and both are moved to another section of the camp to be used as slave labor. *Night* is his account of what Auschwitz was like and of Wiesel's own spiritual response to it.

Hilda Wiesel is one of Eliezer's older sisters, also a survivor. She is mentioned in passing when the narrator describes how the Jews went about their lives heedless of warnings of danger. Before the deportation, his mother was preparing to look for a husband for Hilda.

Sara Wiesel is Elie's mother. She figures little in the narrative. The day before the Jews of Sighet are transported she sends the children to bed early and prepares food for the journey. Eliezer last sees her as she is herded, holding his little sister Tzipora's hand, to the crematoria.

Shlomo Wiesel is Eliezer's father. He ran a store. Wiesel describes him as "a cultured man, rather unsentimental [who] rarely displayed his feelings." He was held in high esteem by the Jews of Sighet, who often sought his advice. He lets opportunities to leave Sighet, before it is too late, pass because he does not have the energy to depart. The head of the occupying German troops summons him to headquarters when they are ready to inform the Jews of their immanent transportation. In Auschwitz he stays near his son and tries to offer what little support he can, but he is overcome by the conditions and dies of dysentery in Buchenwald only weeks before the camp is liberated by the Americans.

Tzipora Wiesel is Elie's adored younger sister. He last sees her in Auschwitz holding his mother's hand as the two of them are herded to their deaths in the ovens.

Yehiel is the brother of the Sighet rabbi. He embraces Eliezer and weeps over their immanent death.

Zalman is a Polish boy marching beside Eliezer on the snowy trek as the evacuation of Buna begins. He had been made to work at the electric parts depot. He suffers terrible stomach cramps as they march. Despite Eliezer's supplication, he falls down in the snow, where he is trampled to death.

Summary and Analysis

1

The story of *Night* begins at the end of 1941 with the encounter between a holy fool, Moishe the Beadle, the handyman and caretaker at the Hasidic synagogue in Sighet, a small town in Transylvania, and Eliezer, a boy of twelve, the narrator and protagonist of the book. He is the child who was fashioned into Wiesel, Nobel laureate and public figure, by the events he will recount in the book and by that very act of recounting.

Night is an autobiographical memoir, an incandescent recollection of a Hasidic, Eastern European Jewish boy's experience of the attempted extermination of all Jewish people by the Germans under Adolph Hitler. *Night* is written in the first person in a novelistic style. In it Wiesel has selected, arranged, and described telling fragments of an overarching experience that, in their totality, re-create that experience and Eliezer's reactions and responses to them.

"Physically" Moishe "was as awkward as a clown." He had "wide dreamy eyes [that] gaz[ed] off into the distance." Usually, instead of speaking, "he sang, or . . . chanted." Wiesel writes that his chants told "of divine suffering, of the Shekhinah in Exile, where, according to Kabbalah, it awaits its redemption," which is "linked to that of man." God's presence, which is called the Shekhinah, depends on humans. Kaballism is a branch of Hasidic Jewish mysticism. In his account of the content of Moishe's chants, Wiesel reveals three things: First, he presents the central idea embedded in the Kabbalah. God has been exiled by the actions of men; God suffers; God's return depends on humankind's return from its own exile, the original expulsion from Paradise. Sin, in other words, affects not only mankind but God also. In losing Paradise, which denotes not only Eden but a loss of the spirit, humankind also lost God, and God lost humankind as well. Sacred study is an attempt to approach the soul's purity and to enter into the realm of purity and redemption, into the realm of God, as if it were an orchard, the lost Eden restored. Pursuing purity is the effort to bring God back from exile. As God takes form within each individual, God is restored outwardly, too. When this miracle is accomplished, evil loses its power and perishes

Second, Wiesel gives meaning to and reason for the unfathomable events of *Night*—God's absence. He is not present. He is exiled. The acts of the Nazis serve as the proof and the manifestation of this godless state. What Eliezer experiences under Nazi persecution is the embodiment of what it means to be exiled from Paradise. It is also the inversion of what he had hoped to obtain through the study of Kabbalah. He finds God by finding the absence of God.

Third, the account of Moishe's chants suggests the legacy that the historical experience Wiesel recounts has burdened him with the work it has implicitly assigned him to do. His work, the book *Night*, is part of the effort to deliver humankind from suffering and to restore God's position. Wiesel is telling, like John Milton, of the lost Paradise, but not before it was lost and how it came to be lost, as Milton does. Wiesel is showing the condition of the world after the severance and alienation have occurred. By taking his reader through Hell, shown to be a human creation—fashioned by human actions, not by divine order or will—he reflects the need to restore Paradise through human acts. That is what it means to be a witness. The act of writing *Night* transforms its author from a survivor into a witness.

In Eliezer's encounter with Moishe, Wiesel is also presenting a dramatic encounter between a man and a boy. The boy desires closer communion with the Divine Spirit. He longs for the purity of soul he believes can be achieved through an encounter with the Divine Spirit. Moishe comes to Elie from that hidden realm as a mortal guide. In this meeting, Wiesel celebrates the continuity of culture, how each generation teaches the essential mysteries embedded in the geography of the spirit's landscape to the succeeding one. Again, this is a task and a responsibility that Wiesel will assume. Moishe initiates Eliezer into the mystery of divine goodness. Moishe also sought to teach the mystery of diabolical evil to the entire Jewish population of Sighet, returning there, after escaping death in a Nazi mass grave. But such teachings were unheeded. In *Night*, Wiesel attempts to continue the work of his teacher.

In contrast to the holy fool, Moishe the Beadle, who is a source of joy to the people of Sighet, Eliezer is a boy torn by a deep religious grief. When he prays three times daily, which he does with avid devotion, he weeps. Moishe notices this and questions him. "Why do you cry when you pray," he asks. Eliezer does not know the reason. Moishe then asks him why he prays. Again the boy does not know, any more than he knows why he lives and breathes. The rest of *Night*, as infused with evil as the events it relates are, because of the horrific nature of that account, is actually the answer to Moishe's question. We live and breathe in order to create, in the only world we have, something as close to Paradise and as far from Hell as we possibly can.

Moishe becomes Eliezer's teacher when the boy wishes to study Kabbalah. His father had told him it was not possible for him to study Kabbalah for two reasons: There were no Kabbalists in Sighet and, according to the sages, one must not begin the study of Kabbalah before the age of thirty. But Moishe the Beadle is adept in Kabbalah, and because he senses depth and seriousness in the boy, begins instruction without mentioning the word *Kabbalah* itself. He explains "that every question possessed a power that was lost in the answer. Man comes closer to God by the questions he asks Him. . . . Man asks and God replies. But we don't understand His replies. . . . Because they dwell in the depths of our souls and remain there until we die. The real answers . . . you will find," the Beadle concludes, "only within yourself." *Night* is Wiesel's act of transcendental questioning, a tripartite interrogation of God's power, of God's goodness, of God's absence.

When Eliezer confesses his sadness at not finding a master in Sighet to instruct him in Kabbalah, Moishe responds by telling him that "[t]here are a thousand and one gates allowing entry into the orchard of mystical truth. Every human being has his own gate. He must not err and wish to enter the orchard through a gate other than his own. That would present a danger not only to the one entering but also for those who are already inside." As if foreshadowing what is to come, Moishe's teaching is a warning. No matter how widespread an event is, its meaning resides in each individual's experience of it. And, within the trajectory of *Night*, it is not only a warning but a guide for mastering events that are themselves overpowering. It is also, because of the Nazi intrusion that defines the book, an admonition not to impose on one's neighbor one's own vision of truth, not to define how one's neighbor ought to be.

2

Structurally, the first section of *Night* introduces the philosophical and spiritual context within which the book's events occur. Instead of entering the radiant realm of the sacred orchard, Eliezer, one among an entire people, enters the realm of evil. The brutality and filth of the transports and the camps reflect the absence of the radiant orchard of the Kabbalah. The episode with Moishe serves as a frame for the rest of the book. Like Dante's pilgrim in the *Divine Comedy*, Eliezer is forced on a journey through Hell in his quest for Paradise. The mystery surrounding the entrance to the radiant orchard is that the gate into it is not a traditional portal but a harrowing challenge. It is the gate of Auschwitz.

The revelation of the pit of Hell as well as of the divine orchard comes from Moishe who announces the challenge and the journey through the damned land that awaits the Jews of Sighet. As a foreign Jew residing in the town, he is deported years before the native Jews are. The Gestapo shot all the Jews they had captured and watched them tumble into the graves they had been forced to dig themselves. Moishe, wounded and left for dead, escapes and returns to tell the others what is occurring, but the Jews of Sighet do not listen. For a brief interlude, things seem normal in Sighet. The Jews are confident the war will end and all will be well. Wiesel's father declines the opportunity to buy an emigration certificate and take his family to Palestine, saying he is too old to start a new life in a distant land. When the time comes that they are taken from their homes and removed from the order and normalcy of their daily lives—first allowed to continue their lives inside the containment of a ghetto and then transported—the Jews experience a ghastly inversion of the biblical exodus from Egypt. Wiesel illuminates that dark moment with a heartbreaking scene of hardly half a page.

After the Germans announced that Jews must prepare to be transported, grief and terror prevailed, and an anguish governed their lives. In a brief dramatic scene, characterized much more by eerie banality than by overt brutality, Wiesel penetrates to the core of the horror. When the Jews must assemble for the deportation, Wiesel is sent to wake one of his father's friends, a man who had "the gaze of a dreamer" and a hunched back "from untold nights spent studying."

"Get up, sir, get up!" [the boy says waking the neighbor]. "You must ready yourself for the journey. Tomorrow you will be expelled, you and your family, you and all the other Jews. Where to? Please don't ask me, sir, don't ask questions. God alone could answer you. For heaven's sake, get up . . ."

He had no idea what I was talking about. He probably thought I had lost my mind.

"What are you saying? Get ready for the journey? What journey? Why? What is happening? Have you gone mad?"

Half asleep, he was staring at me, his eyes filled with terror, as though he expected me to burst out laughing and tell him to go back to bed. To sleep. To dream. That nothing had happened. It was all in jest . . .

My throat was dry and the words were choking me, paralyzing my lips. There was nothing else to say.

At last he understood. He got out of bed and began to dress, automatically. Then he went over to the bed where his wife lay sleeping and with infinite tenderness touched her forehead. She opened her eyes and it seemed to me that a smile crossed her lips. Then he went to wake his two children. They woke with a start, torn from their dreams. I fled.

The narrative is simple, yet its resonance is profound, for the reader knows that this man, lovingly and with a mind that cannot grasp the enormity of the pain that lies before them, is waking his family to begin their journey toward humiliation, torture, grief beyond grief, and death. He is tenderly summoning them to brutality.

The Jews of Sighet were taken away in several convoys. Wiesel and his family were in the last one. Consequently, the boy was able to see the assemblage of Jews on the morning the Hungarian police stormed into the ghetto and, using rifle butts, forced everyone into the streets to begin the deportation. He is even able to bring water surreptitiously to some of those parched with thirst, waiting to begin the exodus, but forbidden to move, even a few paces, back into what had been, so short a time ago, their homes. One of the painfully brilliant elements that recurs in *Night* is the way Wiesel continually keeps every event located not just inside his narrator's perception or the narrowed range of the Jews' experience but how he locates it in the larger world. This dreadful offense to all humanity was happening "under a magnificent blue sky." Wiesel always locates the scene of the action, so that what the reader sees is how isolated and removed the tormented Jews are even from the larger environment, from nature itself, which, nevertheless, still surrounds them.

When *Night's* narrator shows surprise, it is not at the terrible events that befell his family and community but at the naïve responses of the Jews. Once the assembled victims begin their exodus through the streets that were once theirs, outside the homes that are no longer theirs, Wiesel writes, "There was joy, yes, joy." Knowing as he writes what the group of Jews was unable to see or to believe then, he explains, "People must have thought there could be no greater torment in God's hell than that of being stranded here. . . . Anything seemed preferable to that." Wiesel uses irony when he speaks of the way Jews responded to the lot prepared for them. But he does not use irony to describe the evil perpetrated on the Jews or when he writes of those who inflicted the suffering. Wiesel returns immediately to a terse description of the present situation, as he watches the first group from his town being led away, his teachers, his friends, people he had disdained, the chief rabbi, now shorn of his beard: "In everyone's eyes, tears and distress. Slowly, heavily, the procession advanced toward the gate of the ghetto . . . like beaten dogs."

Wiesel then returns to an account of the Jews not yet removed from Sighet. He repeats his father's attempt to speak comforting words, words from another world and another time that once could have made sense but now only mock instead of ease. "Sleep peacefully, children," he says. "Nothing will happen until the day after tomorrow." His mother makes the children "go to bed early," saying it is "to conserve our strength." Wiesel lets the words resonate by themselves without any other comment but "It was to be the last night spent in our house." The reader approaches the text with a knowledge or awareness the characters do not possess or only have an inkling of: They are making the final preparations for the ultimate loss of their identity—death. They are parting with that sense of their humanity that mediates the way others may treat them. Their behavior is no longer theirs. It is no longer voluntary.

When the remaining Jews are marshaled in the street, they are first driven by club-wielding Hungarian police, made to run to the smaller ghetto at the edge of town where they are bunkered in the abandoned apartments of Jews previously transported. Already, before the long journey to the camps and the suffering that awaited them there, the bonds between people were being broken. Eliezer reports, "I went out first. I did not want to look at my parents' faces. I did not want to break into tears." But he could not prevent himself from seeing that his father was crying and that his mother's "face [was] a mask." He sees his little sister Tzipora—in Hebrew the word means "little bird"—"clenching her teeth," bearing the weight "on her back [of] a bag too heavy for her," who "already knew it was useless to complain," and who was bound for immediate extermination at Auschwitz along with her mother.

In the small ghetto, the remaining Jews still deluded themselves, imagining that things would yet be all right for them, that the war would end before they could be deported.

The ghetto was not even guarded. Eliezer's father, weary, refused the help of their former maid, Maria, who was prepared to shelter them in her village. But the next morning, the people were rounded up again and driven to the synagogue, not by Hungarian police this time but by members of the Jewish Council, which had been assigned the job. The synagogue was in shambles, the altar desecrated, the Jews confined inside until the next morning, forced to urinate and defecate in the corners of the *shul*. The Jews walked to the railway station and were forced into cattle cars, stuffed eighty to a car. "One person was placed in charge of every car: if someone managed to escape, that person would be shot." (p. 22)

Inside the cattle car there was no room to lie down or even for everyone to sit. After two days traveling, the train stopped at the Czechoslovakian border where Hungarian police transferred the Jews to German police who collected whatever valuable items the captives might still be carrying. They announced that those who did not cooperate would be immediately shot and then nailed the doors of the cattle cars shut. Wiesel ends the section with the grievous observation, "The world had become a hermetically sealed cattle car." Three sentences earlier he writes, "We had fallen into the trap, up to our necks," bitterly suggesting that the Jews might have avoided imprisonment and death had they taken seriously the threat that had been repeatedly announcing itself and had they overcome the kind of inertia that prevented Elie's father from leading his family to possible safety when the opportunity still existed.

Now inside the cattle car, where "heat ... thirst ... stench ... lack of air, were suffocating" the detainees, Wiesel represents the terrible state of the tragic reversal that has beset their lives with the story of Mrs. Schächter, an emotionally distressed mentally imbalanced woman or a visionary (the distinction was without meaning anymore), who sees, before the train arrives at Auschwitz and its burning furnaces, the consuming flames that await them. "Fire!" she cries ceaselessly. "I see a fire!" It is more than the others in the cattle car can endure. They beat her, gag her, and bind her as "her little boy was crying, clinging to her skirt, trying to hold her hand," vainly trying to calm her. The prisoners in the cattle car explain her screams by saying, "She is hallucinating because she is thirsty. . . . That's why she speaks of flames devouring her." But they cannot silence her. After a few hours, she breaks her bonds and shouts again, "The fire, over there!"

The train stops at Auschwitz, then rolls slowly into the camp. Mrs. Schächter had become quiet until she let out one more scream. "Jews, look! Look at the fire! Look at the flames," she cried. "And as the train stopped," Wiesel writes, "this time we saw the flames rising from a tall chimney into a black sky." The doors of the cattle cars were opened, and the prisoners were beaten and driven out of the cars to see "in front of us, those flames." The air was heavy with "the smell of burning flesh."

3

As they enter the gates at Auschwitz, the men and women are separated from one another. Eliezer and his father are directed to the left, his mother and three sisters to the right. "I did not know," Wiesel writes, "that this was the moment . . . and the place where I was leaving my mother and Tzipora forever." Being separated from his mother begins his transit through Hell, and the death of his father completes it. In between, Wiesel guides the reader through a place where both past and future are completely eradicated and the present is an inescapable and perpetual torment. Although the outcome of the book is known on its first page—its narrator must have survived in order to produce his account—what it does not contain in terms of suspense is amply replaced by the immediacy of horror and fear. Through a series of vignettes, scenes, events, and responses, Wiesel has constructed a narrative of sustained and devastating anxiety, fear, and disbelief. *Night* is a mystical text. At its heart lies an unsolvable puzzle centering on the incomprehensibility of evil, an incomprehensibility that never ceases snagging the mind, engaging and perplexing it, thoroughly frustrating the understanding and defying the rational.

4

The first thirty pages of *Night* are a prologue to its central
scene. The last eighty present an unrelenting account of what
it was like inside the death camps. The power of the book
resides not only in the extreme horror of the events it narrates
but in the very existence of narrative as witness. Through
its account, *Night* becomes a description of a condition of
being. Once he turns left, holding his father's hand, separated
from his mother and sisters, Wiesel presents the emblem of
that condition. "Behind me," he writes, "an old man fell to
the ground. Nearby, an SS man replaced his revolver in its
holster." What is missing in this brief report is mention of the
shooting itself. Individual acts of brutality are not the issue. In
Auschwitz, they are metamorphosed into a pervasive climate.
Apart from the violence inflicted on the inmates, that climate
affects the prisoners and how they interact. Wiesel presents the
first two interactions he experiences, showing the varying and
distorting effects terror can have on individuals.

His first encounter occurs as he walks with the new arrivals in
rows of five to a crossroad where a commandant of the camp—
the infamous doctor Joseph Mengele, Wiesel learns later—waits
to direct each man, pointing with the baton he holds, either
to the right or to the left, to the ovens or to the barracks.
Wiesel is beside an inmate whose gruff manner disguises his
generous spirit. The veteran prisoner asks Eliezer and his father
how old they each are and then corrects their responses. The
boy must say he is eighteen when asked, not fifteen; the man,
forty, not fifty. Their second encounter is with another Jewish
inmate who is a force of anger, directed at the Jews, not at their
oppressors, cursing the Jews for being the victims of oppression.
Some of the younger men, who had managed to hold on to
a knife, when hearing him, whisper together that they must
fight back, attack the guards before they send the prisoners
to the ovens. Among the elders, however, there is reluctance.
They called such rash actions foolish and counseled not to give
up hope, as the prisoners continue to file past Mengele and
receive their sentences. When Eliezer is questioned, he says
he is eighteen; instead of saying he is a student, he says he is a

farmer, imagining how useless in a labor camp a student would be deemed. Mengele points him to the left, the same direction his father is sent. Although he does not know where he is being sent, Eliezer is happy his father is with him. As their line slowly moves forward, other inmates tell them they are headed for the crematorium. Indeed, Eliezer reports he could see "huge flames . . . rising from a ditch." He also sees a truckload of young children thrown into the flaming pit. Wiesel reports then that he said to his father, "I could not believe that human beings were being burned in our times; the world would never tolerate such crimes." His father answers, "The world?" with an interrogative tone of dismissal. "The world is not interested in us. Today, everything is possible, even the crematoria." Here, in his father's words, not in the brutal acts of the Nazis, is the genesis of *Night*. That such things as Wiesel recounts happened was one thing. But that they *could* happen was something of even greater significance. That is the wrong that Wiesel addresses by using his book as a form of testimony, its author a witness to what no one seemed to wish to see.

The ignorance or indifference of the world was the first abandonment Eliezer faced. The second desertion was even worse, particularly for a boy who prayed three times daily, weeping as he did, and who studied the holy and mystic Hebrew texts. It was the absence of God. As the Jews stood advancing to the burning pit, they began chanting the prayer for the dead, the Kaddish, which begins with words glorifying and sanctifying the great name of God. Hearing it, Wiesel reports, "For the first time, I felt anger rising within me. Why should I sanctify his name? The Almighty, the eternal and terrible Master of the Universe, chose to be silent. What was there to thank him for?" As he counted the steps to the pit, Wiesel decided to throw himself against the electrified fence, to take his life rather than allow the extermination. "Face-to-face with the Angel of Death," Eliezer began nevertheless to chant the Kaddish. "Two steps from the pit," the assembled Jews were directed to the left and to the barracks.

Wiesel follows this account of his entry into Auschwitz with the only non-narrative episode in the book, a litany of "nevers."

In eight sentences, each beginning with the word "never," Wiesel pledges never to forget "the small faces of the children whose bodies I saw transformed into smoke under a silent sky," or "the flames that consumed my faith forever," or "those moments that murdered my God and my soul and turned my dreams to ashes."

In the barracks the new inmates are met by the prisoners already there with "sticks in hand, striking anywhere, anyone without reason." The brutality of the death camp is endemic. The new prisoners are forced to strip and stand naked as SS men gauge their strength. In an aside, Wiesel notes that those who appeared most vigorous were assigned to work in the crematoria, mentioning Béla Katz, a young man from Sighet who had arrived a week earlier and "had been forced to place his own father's body into the furnace." Naked, under a rain of blows, carrying only their belts and shoes, the prisoners are herded to a barber where they were shaved completely. Afterwards, some of the new inmates find others they had known before and who were still living and, Wiesel writes with astonishment, "Every encounter filled us with joy—yes, joy." But the mood is of intense sorrow with individuals wandering about weeping and crying out in despair, wishing they had died in their beds rather than "let themselves be brought here." Wiesel ends the section noting that no one thought of those who were no longer among them, who had already, in that limited amount of time since their arrival, been exterminated. No one, in fact, thought at all or even had left the "instinct" for "self-preservation," or "self-defense" or "pride." They had become "souls condemned to wander . . . until the end of time, seeking redemption, seeking oblivion, without any hope of finding either." That is, they had come to reside in Hell.

From this point on, *Night* is a narrative recording one brutality after another, events that would seem indescribable to some and that Wiesel evokes in calm words, clinically chronicling each unthinkable occurence. It is the very calmness of the narrative that lends the text its power. For the Jews, there is morning then evening and then the next day, but it is actually just the same day that has become a perpetual night bringing one horror after another. Time stands still even as it moves forward. The captives are not only locked in the death camp, they are locked in time, subjected to conditions and treatment that eventually overwhelm and claim most of them. Detail by detail, Wiesel relates the living death, the death-in-life that threatened to drain him of the will to live. The only reason those who survived were saved is that, outside the camps, time was not at a standstill and the Nazis could not prevent the war from unfolding as it did.

The day for the prisoners begins at five o'clock in the morning as they are beaten and rousted out of the barracks by *kapos*. Kapos were themselves prisoners, sometimes Jews, sometimes not, often men who had been brutal and criminal in their former lives. Now in a prison society, given a low order of authority, they usually exercised it with fierce brutality. The culture of the camps was such that even people who shared a common victimization were set against each other. Outside the barracks, the prisoners are forced to run naked through the bitter cold to the showers. Before their showers, they were soaked in a foul-smelling barrel of disinfectant. They are brutalized and treated like vermin bearing dreaded disease. Their treatment reflected the Nazi assertion that Jews were not people but noxious invaders, as portrayed in Fritz Hippler's 1940 Nazi propaganda film, *Die Ewige Jude* (*The Eternal Jew*), where images of Jews were juxtaposed with footage of rats swarming sacks of grain. Once disinfected, the prisoners are hurried to long tables piled with clothing. Pants, shirts, and jackets are thrown at them with no thought to proper size. "In a few seconds," Wiesel writes, "we had ceased to be men." He does not write, "we had ceased to be treated like men," but "we had ceased to *be* men." The sentence, thus, refers not only to an exterior phenomenon but to an internal one, to the psychology of the captives. Eliezer realizes that he is not himself: "The student of the Talmud, the child I was, had been consumed by flames." What he had become was "a shape that resembled me." As for his soul, rather than having gained its way, as Eliezer had once sought, into the Kabbalic garden blazing with God, it "had been invaded—and devoured—by a black flame."

As much as *Night* is a representation of the world of the death camps, it is also a reflection of one of the incarcerated.

The death camps were attached to slave-labor camps. A prisoner's physical strength and capacity to do work determined his fate. The weak were incinerated immediately. Those strong enough were worked until they were depleted and then consigned to the furnaces. As the new prisoners were rushed from the showers to the next barracks, Wiesel describes the work he saw other inmates performing, digging holes and carrying sand. But he does not linger on a description of the chores. It is meaningless and oppressive. Nor does he listen to the talk of the other prisoners. He has become a "withered tree in the heart of the desert." As he observes the others around him, so have they. They talk in whispers and the air, "poisoned" with "thick smoke . . . stung the throat." Inside a barracks with a mud floor, the Jews are mustered in rows of five. As they wait for an SS officer, some fall into a sitting position but are made to stand by repeated blows from a kapo. Eliezer momentarily falls asleep on his feet and dreams he is in bed and his mother's hands are caressing his face. Wakened by the cries of kapos demanding that prisoners with new shoes must surrender them, Eliezer thanked God for the mud that caked his shoes and made them look old.

An SS officer enters and "with him, the smell of the Angel of Death." He is tall and brutal, in his thirties and with the look of a criminal. He tells the Jews they are in Auschwitz, were there to work, and if they did not they would be cremated. "Work or crematorium—the choice is yours," he said and left them to the kapos who separated them according to skill. "Locksmiths, carpenters, electricians, watchmakers" were ordered to take a step forward. The rest of the prisoners, including Eliezer and his father were transferred to another barracks and allowed to sit. At that moment, Eliezer's father had an attack of colic, or severe intestinal pain, and approached the kapo, a Roma or gypsy inmate, and speaking in German asked him where the toilets were. After looking at him blankly for a moment, as if coming out of a trance, the man struck Eliezer's father in the face with a blow that sent him falling to the ground, and he "crawled back to his place on all fours." Terrible in itself, the blow to his father causes similar pain for the boy who sees himself sitting passively, unblinking, allowing an assault that "only yesterday" he would have answered by digging "my nails into the criminal's flesh." It is the pain of that change in himself, even more than the assault on his father, that haunts the narrator. Seeing his son's torment, Eliezer's father whispers to him, "It does not hurt," although his cheek burned red where it had been struck.

5

Each day was like the others: prisoners were beaten, tortured, terrorized, humiliated, and made to run from one place to the other. Only minor details changed but not the circumstances nor the overarching tragedy and terror. The transports that had taken Wiesel, his family, and all the Jews of Sighet to Auschwitz had left them at Auschwitz II, an extermination center where, it is estimated, more than one million Jews, 75,000 Poles, and 20,000 Roma were cremated. On a sunny morning in May 1944, Eliezer and his father were mustered along with other inmates in rows of five and driven by the guards with whips and clubs beyond the barbed wire enclosing Auschwitz II, also called Birkenau, to Auschwitz III, a slave-labor camp for the German chemical manufacturing concern, I.G. Farben. Above its entrance gate the German words *ARBEIT MACHT FREI* were inscribed in iron: "Work makes you free."

Arriving at the new camp, the prisoners were once again disinfected and made to take hot showers and then run naked to their barracks. It was at this point that a momentary miracle occurred. A young Polish man was in charge of the barracks, and he addressed the weary prisoners with a smile and kind words, the first that anyone had heard since their ordeal had begun. "Comrades," he began,

> you are now in the concentration camp Auschwitz. Ahead of you lies a long road paved with suffering. Don't lose hope. You have already eluded the worst danger: the selection. Therefore, muster your strength and keep your faith.

We shall all see the day of liberation. Have faith in life, a thousand times faith. By driving out despair, you will move away from death. Hell does not last forever. . . . And now, here is a prayer, or rather a piece of advice: let there be camaraderie among you. We are all brothers and share the same fate. The same smoke hovers over all our heads. Help each other. That is the only way to survive. And now, enough said, you are tired. Listen: you are in Block 17; I am responsible for keeping order here. Anyone with a complaint may come to see me. That is all. Go to sleep. Two people to a bunk. Good night.

For nearly three weeks, it seemed as if things had gotten better. The prisoners were not subject to the customary brutality. They were allowed to wash and were given black coffee in the morning; at noon, a thick but unappetizing soup—which Eliezer would not eat the first day despite his hunger, but which he looked forward to by the third day—and a piece of bread with margarine in the evening. They were allowed to sleep at night and nap during the day. They were allowed to congregate, to talk with one another and even chant Hassidic melodies.

One morning after roll call, having heard that the Jews of Sighet had been brought to the camp, one of the prisoners inquired of a group, "Who among you is Wiesel from Sighet?" Wiesel's father identified himself and the man, whom he did not recognize, explained that he was "Stein from Antwerp. . . . Reizel's husband. Your wife was Reizel's aunt." He had been deported in 1942 and wished to hear if Wiesel knew the status and location of his wife and two boys. Although neither Shlomo nor Eliezer had any news, Eliezer answered that his mother had heard from them and that Reizel and the children were well. It was a lie, told to keep Stein alive. Stein wept with joy. But a week later, when a transport arrived from Antwerp and Stein went to find his family, he learned the truth, that they were dead. "We never saw him again" is all that the narrator says.

In the evenings, as they lay on their cots, some spoke of the "mysterious ways of God, the sins of the Jewish people, and the redemption to come." Comparing himself to the biblical figure of the suffering Job, Wiesel notes that he did not deny the existence of God but "doubted his absolute justice." The men, however, argue that God "wants to see whether we are capable of overcoming our base instincts, of killing the Satan within ourselves." They tell themselves they "have no right to despair," that "if He punishes us mercilessly, it is a sign that He loves us that much more." Only in a time of utter suffering can such a concept arise as a measure of consolation. The prisoners spoke of the "end of the world and the coming of the Messiah." They employ their faith, attempting to look beyond what could be seen. But Eliezer wondered only about where his mother and little sister, Tzipora, were.

At the beginning of the third week in Auschwitz III, the Polish warden of the barracks disappeared. He had been too humane. He was replaced by one more familiar with brutality. The skilled workers, too, had been sent out of the camp to their assigned jobs. Finally, Eliezer, his father, and some hundred others were transferred to Buna. They walked slowly through villages full of people living ordinary lives, "Germans [who] watched us, showing no surprise." The guards teased, flirted with, and kissed the village girls, and the girls giggled. "At least," Wiesel writes, "during all that time, we endured neither shouting nor blows." Also during these three weeks, Wiesel, along with all the other prisoners, was tattooed on the forearm with a number. His was A-7713. "From then on, I had no other name." (p. 42)

6

Wiesel describes Buna, the forced-labor camp at Auschwitz, as looking "as though it had been through an epidemic: empty and dead," with only a few decently dressed inmates visible. He also notes that it was said to be "a very good camp" by those who were already there. The new arrivals, as usual, were sent through the showers, and there they were addressed by the head of the camp, a big, bull-necked man with "thick lips and curly hair" who "gave an impression of kindness" and who ordered food brought for the preadolescent boys among the prisoners.

Everyone was given new clothing and bunked in two tents. The men were assigned to Kommandos, or work gangs, the veteran prisoners telling them which were the better Kommandos and warning against being placed in the construction work gang. Wiesel notes in a wry aside, "As if we had a choice."

Wiesel was among the prisoners put in the charge of a German "tent leader," a man obese to the point of near immobility. His face reminds Wiesel of an assassin's, and his hands resembled the paws of a wolf. He, too, provided extra food for children, and Wiesel notes that some of the camp administrators used the boys to indulge their pedophilic desires. One of the boys, "one of his aids—a tough-looking boy with shifty eyes" offered to get "a good Kommando" for Eliezer providing Eliezer exchange his shoes, still new and in good condition, for a pair the boy would give him in exchange. Eliezer refused, and Wiesel informs the reader that his shoes were soon taken away from him anyhow and that he got nothing for them in exchange.

The day after their arrival at Buna, the new inmates were given a cursory medical checkup and then sent to a dentist who put Eliezer's name on a list because he had a gold crown on one of his teeth. The fourth day after their arrival, the prisoners were mustered in front of the tent where several kapos led the slave gangs to a large shed where an orchestra was playing marching music. Officers were seated at tables carefully recording the number of prisoners leaving the camp in each work detail. Afterwards, the Kommandos, with the musicians no longer playing, marched off to work in step, led by the kapos beating time. Eliezer spoke with several of the musicians as they marched. There was a Dutch violinist, Louis, who complained that the Nazis did not let him play Beethoven because Jews were not permitted to play music by German composers. Juliek was "a Pole with eyeglasses and a cynical smile." Hans was a "young man full of wit." The foreman was Franek, who had been a student in Warsaw. Wiesel briefly names the others accompanying him as they march to work, but it is one of the rare examples of such individuation, of actual naming, in his narrative. For a moment, the sense of brutal isolation and dehumanization that defines an inmate's experience of being in a concentration camp seems to be lifted and the reader is given this short interlude of five adolescents meeting one another and being themselves, in the midst of such extreme degradation. Juliek explains to Eliezer that their work is not dangerous or difficult but that Idek, their kapo "occasionally has fits of madness" and savagely beats whomever he chooses to vent his fury on at that given moment. A German civilian employee explains their work to the inmates, the kapo tells them that the work is important and that those who are lazy will be severely punished. There are French women working along with the male inmates. Eliezer's request that his father work beside him is granted. Yossi and Tibi, brothers from Czechoslovakia, are also in Eliezer's work group. They had belonged to a Zionist organization and knew many Hebrew songs. Eliezer and the two boys hum the melodies as they labor and speak about Palestine, Jerusalem, and the Jordan River, vowing that if they survive they will leave Europe immediately and sail for Haifa. Another of their companions, Akiba Drumer, a mystic, sees in the numerology of a biblical verse assurance that they will be rescued from the camp in a matter of weeks. The prisoners were given each a bar of soap, a washbowl, and a blanket. Their group leader is a Jew named Alphonse who manages to get an extra cauldron of soup for them, for those individuals, as Wiesel adds with a sad bitterness, "who dreamed more of an extra portion of food than liberty." In the mind of a starving prisoner, the reality of food can quickly eclipse the abstraction of freedom.

Amid the horrific conditions, a semblance of stability emerges for Eliezer. Summoned to the dentist again in order to have his gold-capped tooth removed, Eliezer convinces the dentist to delay the extraction. Eliezer succeeds in deferring the procedure again the following time. When he returns for a third time, the dentist's office had been closed, the dentist imprisoned and sentenced to hanging because "he had been dealing in prisoner's gold teeth *for his own benefit*" (emphasis added). Eliezer was glad. His gold tooth, which could be of value to him later, was safe for the time being. He concludes his account of his encounter with the dentist by remarking that "bread" and "soup . . . were my entire life." Like the others he had just mentioned, he had become "nothing but a body. Perhaps even less, a famished stomach [which] alone was measuring time." Wiesel's narrative has become not only an account of the conditions that surround him but also of his own transforming existential state, of what his surroundings make him into.

For Wiesel, the relative ease of life in the slave-labor camp is broken one day when Idek, the kapo, furiously turns on him during a fit and beats him severely. Just as unexpectedly as the upsurge of his rage, the outburst subsides "and [he] sent me back to work as if nothing had happened." Wiesel adds, "as if we had taken part in a game in which both roles were of equal importance." But even this act of inhumanity opens the way for a deferred moment of humanity that resonates in Wiesel's narrative beyond the time of his incarceration. Afterwards, one of the women working beside him, a French woman with whom Eliezer had not spoken because "she did not know German and I did not understand French," wiped the blood from his forehead, smiled mournfully at him, "slipped" him a "crust of bread," and "looked straight into my eyes." The boy sees that she is deeply frightened but wishes to speak with him, and when she finally does speak, it is in "almost perfect German." She tells Eliezer to hold his anger back, to keep his hatred within himself "for another day, for later. The day will come," she tells him, "but not now." And then for the first of only two times in *Night*, Wiesel breaks the narrative unities of time and place. He takes the reader outside the grim, brutal, and deadly confines of Auschwitz. Stepping outside the narrative frame of the camps and its own temporal realities, jumping over "many years," Wiesel situates the reader momentarily in the Paris Métro. It is a bittersweet narrative miracle: in that small interval, that day of which his comforter spoke is revealed. It *will* come to pass. But it is a narrative fact unknowable while Wiesel was inside Buna. Sitting across the aisle from him in the Métro, Wiesel sees "a beautiful woman with dark hair and dreamy eyes," and he knows he has seen those eyes before.

When he speaks to her, the woman says she does not recognize him. He asks her if she was not in Buna in 1944, working in the electrical parts depot. She remembers. They go to a street café and spend the evening swapping accounts. She tells her story, that she is Jewish but had obtained false papers and passed for a non-Jew and consequently was sent to a labor camp rather than to a death camp. No one knew she spoke German. That would have aroused suspicion. But, although it was "imprudent" to speak to him in Buna, she knew "you would not betray me."

The vignette ends, and Wiesel returns to the burden of his account with only the words "Another time" serving as a transition from the civility of sitting on the terrace of a Paris café, as evening falls, back to the relentless brutality of Auschwitz where one violent, painful, humiliating incident follows quickly upon another. Wiesel tells of how Idek beat his father with an iron bar one day as they were loading diesel engines onto freight cars, crying out that the old man was a loafer because he was not working fast enough. Wiesel tells also of the anger he felt in seeing his father beaten but explains that his ire was not directed at the kapo but at his father for not having "avoided Idek's wrath."

Another account of brutalization among the inmates follows. Franek, the foreman of the work gang, demands that Eliezer give him his gold tooth. When Eliezer refuses, "this pleasant and intelligent young man . . . changed. His eyes" shone "with greed." "If you don't give me your crown," he tells Eliezer, "it will cost you much more." On his father's advice, Eliezer maintains his refusal. Franek begins his campaign to get Eliezer's gold crown by brutalizing his father, giving him daily beatings since the old man is unable to march precisely in time, and the inmates march whenever they go from place to place. Eliezer tries, to no avail, to teach his father to march. Finally, he accedes to Franek's demand and must surrender not only his gold-capped tooth but give a ration of bread to the man who will pull the tooth. If he does not, Franek explains he will "break your teeth by smashing your face." After Franek gets Eliezer's tooth, he "became pleasant again," even sometimes giving the boy extra soup.

Horror follows horror. Next Wiesel tells of what he calls "a novel experience," one which begins almost as an interlude of comparative freedom but which becomes an account of debauchery ending with a staggering display of brutality. One Sunday morning, when Wiesel's Kommando was not required to work, Idek insisted, nevertheless, on marching them to the depot. Putting Franek in charge, and telling them to make themselves busy as they liked, he disappeared. But they had nothing to do and wandered through the depot hoping perhaps to find food that civilian workers might have left. Eliezer wandered to the back of the building. Hearing sounds coming from a side room, he "moved closer" and saw "Idek and a young Polish girl, half naked, on a straw mat." Realizing that a hundred prisoners had been moved "so that he could copulate with this girl," Eliezer laughed at the sight and startled Idek, who lunged at Eliezer, took him by the throat and sent him back to his place after saying he would pay for having seen what he did. That evening at roll call Eliezer was called out of the ranks by his number and was given twenty-five hard lashes with a whip. He fainted, coming to after being doused with cold water. When he was ordered to stand he could not and was lifted to his feet and supported by two inmates who brought him to face Idek. Wiesel reports that he saw nothing but could only think that his father was suffering even more than he, seeing all this and powerless to do anything. After Idek warned him that if he told anyone what he had seen he would receive five times as much and asked him if he "understood," Eliezer nodded "endlessly."

The next episode concerns what happened inside the camp as American bombers strafed the factories. Wiesel takes the reader through the events of the day. Half the group, his father among them, were at work. The group Eliezer was in stayed behind and was resting when the bombing started. All inmates were confined to their blocks, the guard towers emptied, the current in the fences turned off, and SS officers had orders to shoot anyone outside their blocks. Almost in slow motion, Wiesel describes how one prisoner crawled on his belly through the deserted street to a cauldron of soup that stood unguarded in the roadway. The other prisoners look on with fear and envy, all of them consumed by hunger, at the man risking his life in quest of a little soup. When the famished man finally manages to pull himself to his feet and reaches into the cauldron, he is shot and falls dead beside it. Wiesel notes that, despite the danger to themselves from the bombing, the inmates were not afraid but glad to see the camp being bombed. Eliezer's father returned, uninjured, with his detail after the raid. While several buildings had been destroyed, the depot itself had not been hit.

7

Night is divided into nine sections, and within each of these nine sections, there are many also unnumbered subsections. It is at the end of the fourth section, in its last two subsections that the climax of *Night* occurs, even though Wiesel's narrative is little more than half finished. Wiesel prepares for the climactic event by recounting, in the preceding section, the story of the hanging of an inmate accused of stealing during the air raid. Wiesel presents the scene in detail. The ten thousand inmates of the camp were mustered, encircled by SS troops. The guards in the towers held machine guns aimed at the prisoners. Two SS men brought a prisoner, a boy, to the gallows. A judge announced his crime and pronounced his punishment. He refused to be blindfolded. With the rope around his neck, before the chair was pulled out from under his feet, he cried out, "Long live liberty! My curse on Germany." The prisoners watching were ordered all to remove their caps in respect and then to put them on again. Finally, the prisoners, block by block were made to file past the hanged boy and look into "his extinguished eyes, the tongue hanging from his gaping mouth." Wiesel concludes the section with the bitterly ironic observation, "I remember that on that evening, the soup tasted better than ever," showing not only how desensitized the extreme and cold brutality of their treatment had made the inmates but also how it focused them intensely, too, on their own animal hunger and self-centered wish to stay alive.

Were this the only such event Wiesel had chosen to recount, it would have been sufficient. But it is followed by another that is made to take on symbolic meaning fraught with the power of a dark revelation. Embedded in Wiesel's narrative, too, are otherwise unreported acts about life in concentration camps. The brutality and despair Wiesel recounts functioned like the air, the oxygen, the inescapable environment of the camps. But within the confines of that terrible world many forms of adaptation developed. The hierarchy among prisoners, where some served as kapos and some as the supervisory *oberkapos*, established positions of privilege and domination. Inmates chosen to be group leaders, as well as nonincarcerated administrators inside the camps often had young men, boys often, called pipels, who were servants to them and often sexual partners, too. Wiesel notes that in general pipels "were hated" and "often displayed greater cruelty than their elders. I once saw," he continues, as illustration, "one . . . a boy of thirteen beat his father for not making his bed properly. As the old man quietly wept, the boy kept yelling, 'If you don't stop crying instantly, I will no longer bring you bread.'"

In the climactic scene, however, Wiesel tells of the pipel of a kind Dutch oberkapo. He never beat or insulted any of the seven hundred men he supervised and "all loved him like a brother." His pipel, too, "was beloved by all." Of this beautiful and delicate boy, Wiesel writes, "his face was the face of an angel in distress." After a power failure at the camp, undoubtedly an act of sabotage, the Gestapo was called in to investigate. The officers not only concluded that it was the work of the Dutch oberkapo, but they found a large cache of weapons in his block. He was arrested, tortured, refused to speak, and was taken to the extermination camp in Auschwitz. His pipel remained in Buna in solitary confinement. He was tortured, too, and like the Dutchman, refused to speak. Along with two other inmates, he was condemned to death.

Those are the circumstances behind the event Wiesel proceeds now to rehearse, focusing no longer on what might be called the politics of death but on its pure existential essence. He presents a terrible spectacle that ascends to the order of a religious event. Wiesel constructs a scene in which a slight, beloved, tender, and beautiful boy is hanged, dying silently, not hurling invectives at his tormentors nor blessing liberty but enshrouded in his own silent and distressed beauty, a figure of the extreme suffering of death-in-life, particularly because he did not die shortly after the chair was pulled out from under his legs. "He remained for more than half an hour," Wiesel reports, "lingering between life and death, writhing before our eyes." It is then that the comparison with Christ is made, giving to the Jewish victims the ontological standing and suffering of the Christian Savior.

> "Where is merciful God, where is He?" someone behind me was asking. . . .
> "For God's sake, where is God?"
> And from within me, I heard a voice answer:
> "Where He is? This is where—hanging here from this gallows . . ."

The fifth section of *Night* begins with a reference to time and the seasons. Summer is ending and the end of the Jewish year, which occurs sometime in September in the Gregorian calendar, is approaching. Wiesel describes the congregation of "some ten thousand men" in Buna gathered to pray on the last day of the year—noting the dreadful irony that informed the word *last* since it might actually be any one of the prisoner's final day. Interwoven with his description of the service and the congregants, Wiesel reveals his anguished and angry responses: "Blessed be God's name? . . . why would I bless Him? . . . Because He caused thousands of children to burn in His mass graves?" Like the biblical Abraham, Eliezer argues with God and becomes his accuser: "Look at these men whom You have betrayed," he utters in his mind, "allowing them to be tortured, slaughtered, gassed, and burned, what did they do? They pray before you. They praise your name." Eliezer remembers his boyhood in Sighet when he "believed that the salvation of the world depended on every one of my deeds, on every one of my prayers." In Buna, having been through Auschwitz, "now, I no longer pleaded for anything. . . . My eyes had opened and I was alone . . . in a world without God, without man. Without love or mercy. I was nothing but ashes now.... I felt like an observer, a stranger."

The New Year's service ends with the Kaddish, the mourner's prayer for the dead. In this instance, Wiesel notes that the congregants said the Kaddish for themselves as well as for their parents or their children. After the service, which Wiesel calls a "surreal moment," Eliezer looked for his father, "afraid of having to wish him a happy new year in which I no longer believed." Instead, when he found him, silently he kissed his father's hand and felt tears on his own, not knowing whether they were his or his father's. Then the bell that signaled bedtime sounded. Parting from his father, Eliezer "looked up . . . trying to glimpse a smile or something like it on his [father's] stricken face." But he only saw defeat there.

Yom Kippur, the Jewish Day of Atonement given over to suffering and penitence, follows soon after Rosh Hashanah, the New Year. It is a day of prayer and fasting, when God is addressed and implored on the sinner's behalf to grant a respite, to allow one more year of life to the supplicant, forgiven, released from the burden of past sin, free to begin anew on a path of virtue and righteousness. But how could this day with its discipline and rituals, with its practice of fasting and bearing voluntary suffering, apply to Jews in Auschwitz, where every day was more fraught with grief than any Yom Kippur, with suffering and punishment beyond even the worst sins any of them ever had to atone for? That was the question that the Jews of Buna discussed as the Day of Atonement approached. In addition, there was a practical issue they debated, fasting itself. The Jews in the camp were famished already, all but fasting every day. Eliezer, following his father's injunction against fasting and because of his own distance from God—"I no longer accepted God's silence"—"swallowed my ration of soup" and "nibbled on my crust of bread," and, as he did, instead of being fed, "deep inside . . . felt a great void opening."

The New Year and the Day of Atonement were followed by the announcement that a new "selection" was about to be made. All Jews deemed unfit by the camp commander, Joseph Mengele, were to be exterminated. Eliezer and his father at the time were bunkered in different blocks and working in different labor gangs. The news of the upcoming selection caused a general anxiety in the camp, but Eliezer had viable reason to worry specifically about whether his father would survive the selection. In the face of impending death, Wiesel shows the routines of Buna, choosing particular details that collectively offer a portrait of life continuing amid horror. Twelve hours a day, Eliezer "hauled heavy slabs of stone." "The head of my new block was a German Jew, small with piercing eyes." "No one was allowed to leave the block after the evening soup." Everyone knew that it meant selection. "After soup, we gathered between the bunks." (Time seems to be measured out in bowls of soup. A count of the frequency with which the word *soup* appears in *Night* would show just how pervasive starvation was in the camp—how central the little ration of what in any other situation would have been unpalatable was.) The long-term residents of the camp tease the newcomers telling them now "this is paradise compared to what the camp was two years ago. . . . No water, no blankets, less soup and bread. At night, we slept almost naked and the temperature was thirty below." They laugh when Eliezer begs them to be quiet. And some are quiet, too, "the old men . . . in their corner, silent, motionless, hunted-down . . . praying."

Before the "selection," the block leader, a man who had been incarcerated since 1933, who "had already been through all the slaughterhouses, all the factories of death," as "his voice quivered," addressed his group of prisoners, Eliezer among them, wishing them luck, advising them to "try to move your limbs, give yourself some color," to try to look healthy and strong. It is as if they were going into an audition or a job interview. As you would tell someone in such a situation, "Don't be nervous," he concluded, "most important, don't be afraid." "That was," Wiesel comments with an irony leavened by the distance of years after, "a piece of advice we would have loved to be able to follow."

Wiesel's narrative strategy throughout *Night*, what makes it a compelling experience for readers, is that he reinserts himself into Auschwitz, relives it, undergoes it again, rather than only reporting it from a safe distance, as if to say there can be no distance, nor any safety in distance. Wiesel details the events that made up the "selection." He runs naked before Mengele, so fast that he cannot see if his number is recorded or not, transcribing for the reader the anxious thoughts that flew through his mind as he rushed past the Angel of Death. The block leader announces afterward that no one from his bunk has been selected. Several days later, when he musters his group to read off the names of the ten who have been selected, he can do nothing. Eliezer's father, too, has been selected, even though he thought he had not been written down. "Me too, me too," he laments. "What are we going to do?" Eliezer asks "anxiously." But there is nothing to do but hope. Hardly believing himself, Eliezer's father says, "It's not certain yet. There's still a chance." As if contradicting his feeble reassurance, he gives Eliezer his knife and spoon, saying he won't need them anymore. Taking them, Eliezer says, "My inheritance." The kapo shouts out the order to march and to "the din of military music," Eliezer leaves his father behind. In the evening, after the agony of a day "sick at heart," during which his fellow prisoners treated him with the especial kindness one must confer on an orphan, Eliezer finds his father still among the living. "Were there still miracles on this earth? . . . He had passed the second selection."

Akiba Drumer, the mystic who had predicted liberation through a numerological study of sacred text, did not survive the selection. Even before it, he had become entirely dispirited. So had "a rabbi from a small town in Poland." "Old and bent . . . lips constantly trembling . . . always praying . . . one day he said . . . , 'It's over. God is no longer with us. . . . I know. No one has the right to say things like that. . . . But what can someone like myself do? . . . I . . . have eyes and I see what is being done here. Where is God's mercy? Where's God? How can I believe, how can anyone believe in this God of Mercy?'" When Akiba Drumer is taken away to be killed, Wiesel laments that "if only he could have kept his faith in God, if only he could have considered this suffering a divine test, he would not have been swept away by the selection." But saying this seems only to be Wiesel's attempt to grasp at a straw, for such was not his own strength. Frequently, throughout *Night*, Eliezer has indicated, regarding himself, that faith in God was not his strength either. Indeed, it was not his faith in God, it seems, that fed his will to live but his attachment to and concern for his father. With bitter irony, Wiesel concludes the section by noting that, after Akiba Drumer's removal, "terrible days" followed. The inmates "received more blows than food. The work was crushing." They forgot to say Kaddish, the prayer for the dead, for Akiba Drumer.

With the onset of winter, "glacial wind" made everything worse. It "lashed us like a whip." The veterans of the camp seem to take pleasure at having endured such things before and tease the newcomers. Christmas and New Year's Day come and go. The work is agony. The stones the prisoners had to move were so cold their fingers stuck to them. In January, Eliezer's foot "began to swell from the cold," and he went to the infirmary where "a great Jewish doctor" told him he would have to operate in order to prevent having to amputate toes or, later, the leg.

"Being in the infirmary," Wiesel notes, "was not bad at all." There was better food, real beds and white sheets." In the bed next to Eliezer's was a Hungarian Jew who spoiled his comfort, warning the boy that there was nothing safe about the infirmary, that the "selection" from within the infirmary was greater than from the rest of the camp. He advises Eliezer to leave the infirmary. But the boy stays, worrying about what his neighbor has said, but worrying equally about the man's motives. The doctor drains pus from the sole of Eliezer's foot and assures him that in two weeks he will be fine. But two weeks were not to be had. Two days after the operation, there were rumors throughout the camp that the Russian Army "was racing toward Buna." Although rumors of liberation had been common, this one seemed to be accurate. The prisoners had heard cannon fire sounding throughout the night. Dampening Eliezer's hope, his neighbor in the next bed warned him not to delude himself, that Hitler had pledged to "annihilate all Jews before the clock strikes twelve." In wrath Eliezer responds, "What do you care what he said? Would you want us to consider him a prophet?" The man's answer, cynical as it is, has a solid foundation in the facts of the Jew's plight. "I have more faith," he said, "in Hitler than in anyone else. He alone has kept his promises, all his promises, to the Jewish people."

The afternoon of the day that exchange took place, it was announced that Buna was being evacuated and that the Jews were to be marched out of the camp and delivered to one of the camps inside Germany. The sick, however, would be allowed to remain behind in the infirmary. But speculation outpaced facts, and the inmates spread additional rumors that the camp would be blown up after the evacuation or that everyone left behind would be delivered to the crematoria's fires. Hearing the news of the approaching Red Army, Eliezer runs out of the infirmary to seek his father, more intent on remaining with him, whether their decision would be to stay or to go. Although the doctor assured Eliezer that his father could stay in the infirmary, too, his father decides on evacuation, asking the boy if he will be able to walk. Wiesel notes then that after the war, he learned that those who stayed behind were liberated by the Russians two days after the evacuation.

With doubled rations of bread and margarine, dressed in as much clothing as they could find in the storeroom, driven out in the blistering cold and with armed SS men running beside them, shooting any who were too slow or who fell under the feet of the others, the prisoners ran like automatons. Eliezer, unable to find a shoe big enough for his inflamed foot, wrapped it in a swath torn from his blanket. Wiesel's narration of this terrible journey from Buna to Buchenwald is an account of deaths, betrayals, and his own unrelenting dedication to stay with his father, to stay alive for his sake and to keep him alive, how they slept by turns in the snow and how he beat his father back to life from the margins of death, when the old man's seemingly lifeless body was about to be thrown with other corpses off a convoy train.

He tells of Zalman, who succumbed to the agony of stomach cramps, fell to the ground, and was trampled to death. He tells of Rabbi Eliahu, searching, inquiring for his son. After Eliezer tells him he has not seen him, he recalls that he did see him, running ahead of his father, to free himself, Eliezer imagines, when the old man lagged behind, of his filial burden, in the hope of saving himself. Eliezer prays to the "God in whom I no longer believed" to "give me strength never to do what Rabbi Eliahu's son has done." He tells of being trapped within a mound of dying bodies in a Nazi camp in the Polish town of Gleiwitz, of finding his old friend from Buna, Juliek, the violinist from Warsaw, buried under him, but still alive, and how they struggled to extricate themselves from the mound of bodies, Juliek carrying the violin he managed to bring along with him. He tells of how Juliek played a section of the violin concerto by Beethoven, something the Nazis had forbidden Jews to do, to an audience of the dead and the nearly dead and how Juliek himself soon lay dead beside his broken violin. He tells of traveling, a hundred men to a car, through German villages and of how townspeople tossed pieces of bread to the Jews in the cattle cars and watched as people watch animals at a zoo, the way the inmates tore at each other to grab morsels of bread. And for the second time in *Night*, Wiesel goes outside the boundaries of the narrative. Unlike the anecdote of his meeting in the Métro with the young woman who had succored him after a beating in Buna, he now tells of "an elegant Parisian lady" who "took great pleasure" from the deck of a ship docking in Aden "throwing coins to the 'natives,' who dove to retrieve them," sometimes "fighting in the water" for them. He focuses on two children vying for the coins, "one trying to strangle the other." When he begs her not to throw any more coins, she responds with blind hauteur, "Why not? I like to give charity." Returning to the main narrative, Wiesel tells how he saved his father from another "selection" by causing a confusion that allowed a number of inmates in addition to his father to evade death for another moment. And he tells of how, starving and with no food, and forbidden even to bend down, lines of prisoners ate spoonfuls of snow from the shoulders of the prisoners in front of them.

When the convoy of prisoners finally reached Buchenwald, it was January of 1945. Twelve of the one hundred who had been in the wagon carrying Eliezer and his father were still alive. Wiesel's account of his time in Buchenwald describes his father's final suffering and death, his dysentery and his burning fever, his pitiful begging for water, the assaults he suffered from other prisoners who stole his bread and beat him because in his incontinence he made their barracks even more foul than it already was, and of the beatings of the SS men who tried to silence his death cries, beatings that Eliezer witnessed with a numb passivity. It is, collaterally, the account of Eliezer's guilt, of his struggle to stay near his father even when he knew it would improve his chances of survival to abandon him. And although he did not desert him, Eliezer compares himself to Rabbi Eliahu's son, feeling insufficient to the impossible task set for him, feeling that his father "had called out to me and I had not answered." But, although Wiesel makes no allusion to it, the reader familiar with the story of the fall of Troy may think of him more like the Trojan hero Aeneas escaping the burning city carrying Anchises, his aged father, on his back. After Eliezer finds his father gone from his plank in the barracks on the morning of January 29, he says of his father's death, "Free at last!" Undoubtedly, the ambiguity of the reference is not accidental.

The ninth and final section of *Night* is brief. After his father's death, Eliezer was transferred to the children's block, thought neither of his father or mother, remained idle, and thought only of food, even dreamed of soup. On April 5, all Jews were summoned to the central assembly grounds of Buchenwald, but on the way they were warned by other prisoners to go back to their barracks, that the Nazis intended to shoot them all. Although Wiesel has not yet mentioned anything about it, except glancingly in the account of the Dutch barracks leader and his angelic pipel who was hanged, now he reveals that there was a resistance movement in Buchenwald, and at this time, when captives were being evacuated daily and probably exterminated, "the resistance movement decided . . . to act.

Armed men appeared from everywhere. Bursts of gunshots. Gerenades exploding. . . . The battle did not last long. . . . The SS had fled and the resistance had taken charge of the camp." On April 10, at six o'clock in the evening, "the first American tank stood at the gates of Buchenwald."

Their "first act as free men," Wiesel writes, was to eat. No one, he says, thought of revenge, only of bread. It is unclear whether this observation is a commendation or a reproach. On April 11, Wiesel reports, some of the young men went into Weimar, the German city famous as the birthplace of Goethe, the great nineteenth-century German writer, "to bring back some potatoes and clothes—and to sleep with girls." Three days later, Eliezer fell ill and "spent two weeks between life and death." Once he was stronger and able to get out of bed, he concludes his narrative, for the first time since being wrenched away from Sighet, seeing himself in a mirror. What he saw, he says, was a corpse contemplating him with a "look in his eyes [that] has never left me." It is the person he had become in the camps regarding him, who, in all the things Wiesel has done since then, has never stopped looking at him, measuring him, exacting labors from him, the chief of which is this book.

Critical Views

Of all the crimes by the Nazis, surely the most unforgivable is the internment and murder of so many children. It has been calculated that a million Jewish children perished during the war. Yet many children managed to survive years in the death camps, and now, only in their late twenties and early thirties, have turned out to be the most effective personal historians of life under the Nazis. This is the generation of Anne Frank (who would now have been thirty-one), and the young Spaniard Michel del Castillo, who in that unforgettable memoir *A Child of Our Time* described what it was like to be a child in Buchenwald.

Children who went through such experiences and survived have more than anyone else been able to express the fundamental violation of human dignity committed by the Nazis. The battle-weary soldiers, the superficially experienced journalists, the hardened politicals—none of these has been able to convey, with the same innocence, the full atrocity of the camps. And perhaps only a few of the children themselves felt innocent enough, after constantly being told that they were guilty of being outside the German law, to resent the Nazis at all. But what has made a few good books possible is the fact that some of these children were still so impressionable and trusting that the terrible experiences of the camps were stored up subconsciously in their minds. Only now, in our relatively "peaceful" period, have such memories risen to the surface. Yet such experiences can become curiously unreal even to people constantly obsessed by them, and remarkably vivid as these memoirs are, they often betray the writer's fear that he may be describing a hallucination.

The author of this piercing memoir of life in Auschwitz, Birkenau, and Buchenwald was only sixteen when the war ended for him in April, 1945. By that time he had been separated from his mother and sisters, whom he never saw again; he had seen his own father, after surviving so many "selections," smashed to death. He had lived in Auschwitz with the constant odor of burning human flesh; he had seen children, still alive, thrown into the crematoria; he had seen starving men, in the cattle cars transporting them from one camp to another, fighting each other to death over pieces of bread negligently tossed them by German civilians. There are details in his book which can be read only with fresh astonishment at the unflagging cruelty of the Nazis and the peculiarly sadistic frivolity of those who directed this vast system of human extermination. The infamous SS doctor, Mengele, who quickly "selected" those who were to be gassed from the terror-stricken crowds running and stumbling before his eyes, would motion people to death with a conductor's baton! And there is one particular scene which has already made this book famous in Europe. A young boy, after days of being tortured in an attempt to make him reveal where a Dutch prisoner had hidden arms, was put up on the gallows to be hanged. His body was too light and so he kept strangling in front of the thousands of prisoners who had been summoned to watch the execution and who were marched past the gallows. As they went by, Wiesel heard a man asking, "Where is God now?" And he heard himself thinking—"Here He is—He is hanging here on this gallows . . ."

It is this literal "death of God" as absolute emptiness in the soul, the blackness that in his mind means that there is no longer any light from a divine source, that Wiesel experienced most in the endless night of Auschwitz. What makes his book unusual and gives it such a particular poignancy among the many personal accounts of Nazism is that it recounts the loss of his faith by an intensely religious young Jew who grew up in an Orthodox community of Transylvania. To the best of my knowledge, no one of this background has left behind him so moving a record of the direct loss of faith on the part of a young boy.

Night is about a world so unreal that often indeed it reads like a nightmare. Wiesel would be the first to admit its seeming unreality; often enough it must seem unreal to him. But the book satisfies us as a human document; it brings us back to the world we all know, through the crisis of faith that it describes. The Book of Job is the most universally understood part of the Bible, and the young Wiesel's embittered interrogation of Providence unites, as it were, the ever-human Job to the history of our own time; it recalls that peculiarly loving and scolding intimacy with God which is the most powerful single element in the history of the Jews.

It was Wiesel's religious background that originally interested the French Catholic writer François Mauriac in this book. When Wiesel, now an Israeli newspaperman, came to interview Mauriac, the latter described the ineradicable impression that had been made on Mme. Mauriac as she watched the trainloads of Jewish children being deported from Austerlitz Station in Paris. When Mauriac spoke of how often he thought of these children, Wiesel replied, "I was one of them." Mauriac's preface to the book is singularly beautiful, and though a devout Christian, he describes the martyrdom of the Jews in terms reminiscent of the death of Christ. He too sees the Jewish experience under Nazism in Biblical terms. He describes young Wiesel as "a Lazarus risen from the dead," and, recalling Nietzsche's cry that "God is dead," expresses his compassionate understanding of why a boy in Auschwitz should have thought that "God is dead, the God of love, of gentleness, of comfort, the God of Abraham, of Isaac, of Jacob, has vanished forevermore, beneath the gaze of this child, in the smoke of a human holocaust exacted by Race, the most voracious of all idols." Mauriac's preface is written with that charity and intellectual passion which is the particular mark of French Catholic writers. The magnanimity and literary distinction of his few pages puts into relief the rather delicate literary achievement of Wiesel himself, who in recounting these atrocious early experiences makes one realize how difficult it is for a victim to do full justice to the facts.

Yet Mauriac's preface, beautiful as it is, misses the dramatic human element, the Job-like accusations that actually unite Wiesel to the religion of his fathers. On the Jewish New Year service in Auschwitz, when ten thousand prisoners said with one voice, "Blessed be the name of the Eternal," the young boy defied the Divinity, Whom he had come to think of as blind and deaf: ". . . but why should I bless Him? In every fiber I rebelled. Because He had had thousands of children burned in His pits? Because He kept six crematories working night and day, on Sundays and feast days? Because in His great might He had created Auschwitz, Birkenau, Buna, and so many factories of death? How could I say to Him: 'Blessed art Thou, Eternal, Master of the Universe, Who chose us from among the races to be tortured day and night, to see our fathers, our mothers, our brothers, end in the crematory?' . . .

"This day I had ceased to plead. I was no longer capable of lamentation. On the contrary, I felt very strong. I was the accuser, God the accused. My eyes were open and I was alone—terribly alone in a world without God and without Man . . . I stood amid that praying congregation, observing it like a stranger.

"The service ended with the Kaddish [prayer for the dead]. Everyone recited the Kaddish over his parents, over his children, over his brothers, and over himself."

To Mauriac, this loss of faith seems unnecessary as well as tragic, and he wishes, in effect, that Wiesel could see all these immense losses in our time from a Christian point of view. Mauriac feels that the deportation of children touches upon "the mystery, of iniquity whose revelation was to mark the end of one era and the beginning of another. The dream which Western man conceived in the eighteenth century, whose dawn he thought he saw in 1789, and which, until August 2, 1914, had grown stronger with the progress of enlightenment and the discoveries of science—this dream vanished finally for me before those trainloads of little children." Mauriac is a great soul in our time. But less gifted, less hopeful, and even pathetic as the young Wiesel is, there is a positive strength to his complaints against God that Mauriac may have missed.

The accusation of God is of someone very real to Wiesel. The dialogue continues. It is exactly because of a child's demand for justice, because of his demand on God, because of his insistence that the consummation has not yet been reached and that history remains imperfect, that the book is so effective. Faith is often hard to talk about. Franz Kafka even said that he who has faith *cannot* talk about it. What counts may be not always one's explicit assent to faith or to non-faith, but the immense confrontation of history, the demand that we make of it as the only ground on which justice may yet show itself. I don't think that I shall soon forget the picture of this young boy standing on a mound of corpses, accusing God of deserting His creation.

ELLEN S. FINE ON FATHER-SON RELATIONS IN *NIGHT*

If the nocturnal forces of death envelop and endure, miraculously, from within the depths of the Holocaust universe surges the will to live. Father and son struggle to remain human, acting as lifelines for each other. They fight to keep alive by mutual care and manage to create a strong bond between them in the most extreme of circumstances. Yet competition for survival causes a conflict between self-interest and concern for the other. Close ties break down in the kingdom of *Night* and even the solidarity built up between Eliezer and his father is undermined by feelings of anger and ambivalence brought about by Nazi techniques specifically designed to destroy human relationships.

"A residue of humanism persists illogically enough in our world, where there is a 'void' at the center of things," Wylie Sypher observes, in *Loss of the Self in Modern Literature and Art*. For a child of fifteen entering the perverse world of the concentration camp, the "residue of humanism" is the presence of his father. Separated from his mother and three sisters upon their arrival at Birkenau, Eliezer becomes obsessed with the need to hold on tightly to his father's hand, the only object of life in a universe where every moment holds the possibility of death. "My hand shifted on my father's arm. I had one thought—not to lose him. Not to be left alone." Warned by an anonymous prisoner to lie about their ages, the fifteen-year-old boy and the fifty-year-old man instantly become eighteen

58

and forty, and are thus able to follow Dr. Mengele's wand to the left-hand column (life) instead of the right-hand one (crematoria).

The fear of being torn apart from his last family link haunts the narrator throughout the book. During the "leveling" process, as he is being stripped bare of all possessions, he is fixated on one thought—to be with his father. Later, when the boy is recovering from a foot operation in the Buna hospital and finds out that the camp is about to be evacuated, he runs outside into the deep snow, a shoe in his hand because his foot is still swollen, and frantically searches for his father: "As for me, I was not thinking about death, but I did not want to be separated from my father. We had already suffered so much together; this was not the time to be separated." Upon arrival in Buchenwald after the long tortuous convoy in the open wagons, Eliezer is again haunted by the familiar fear and fiercely clutches his father's hand.

This obsession to hold on to the father has been interpreted by the French scholar André Neher as juvenile. He feels that "Elie remains a small, dependent child in spite of the overabundant maturity resulting from his experience." However, if the gesture of grasping the hand is somewhat childlike, and the son's vow never to be severed from his father has a desperate tone, the primary relationship between father and son appears to be more an interdependency based upon mutual support in the midst of surrounding evil. Father and son, joined together in front of the sacrificial altar, recalls the biblical story of Abraham and Isaac (the *Akeda*), described by Wiesel in *Messengers of God* with the emphasis on commitment in a world threatened by destruction: "And the father and son remained united. Together they reached the top of the mountain; together they erected the altar; together they prepared the wood and the fire." Wiesel cites a text form the Midrash in which the biblical pair are envisages as "victims together," bound by their communal offering.

Until the last pages of *Night*, reciprocal devotion sustains both Eliezer and his father and is linked to the recurring Wieselian theme of rescue—saving the life of another human being and thereby saving one's own. The narrator reports several instances during which his father's presence stops him from dying. When Eliezer files past the fiery pits on the first hallucinatory night in Auschwitz, he has thoughts of suicide. He is deterred from killing himself by the voice of his father who tells him that humanity no longer cares about their fate, and that at this time in history everything is permitted. The father's voice, though sad and choked, represents a life force, which combats the all-encompassing blackness.

During the long march from Buna to Gleiwitz, the prisoners are forced to gallop through the snow, and Eliezer, pained by his throbbing foot, is again drawn to death as an escape from suffering. Once more the paternal presence helps him to resist the appeal of death. Because he feels that his father needs him, the son does not have the right to succumb. His will to survive is ultimately linked to the existence of his father:

> Death wrapped itself around me till I was stifled. It stuck to me. I felt that I could touch it. The idea of dying, of no longer being, began to fascinate me. Not to exist any longer. Not to feel the horrible pains in my foot. . . . My father's presence was the only thing that stopped me . . . I had no right to let myself die. What would he do without me? I was his only support.

After seventy kilometers of running, as morning approaches, the survivors are allowed to rest. The narrator sinks into the soft snow, but his father persuades him to go into the ruins of a nearby brick factory, since to sleep in the snow means to freeze to death. The open shed, too, is crusted with a thick cold carpet enticing its weary victims, and Eliezer awakes to the frozen hand of his father patting his cheeks. A voice "damp with tears and snow" advises the boy not to be overcome by sleep. Eliezer and his father decide to watch over each other: they exchange vows of protection, which bind them together in revolt against the death that is silently transforming their sleeping comrades into stiffened corpses.

Later on, when the men pile on top of each other in the barracks of Gleiwitz, Eliezer struggles to rid himself of an unknown assassin slowly suffocating him with the massiveness of his weight. When he finally liberates himself and swallows a mouthful of air, the boy's first words are to his father whose presence is acknowledged by the sound of his voice, "a distant voice, which seemed to come from another world." The voice once again is a lifeline, a reassurance against death. Yet the otherworldiness of the father's speech suggests that he is beginning to lose hold of his vital forces; eternal night beckons to him.

The last time the father rescues the son is in the open cattle car shuttling the victims from Gleiwitz to Buchenwald. On the third night of the trip, the narrator suddenly wakes up: somebody is trying to strangle him. He musters enough strength to cry out the one word synonymous with survival— "Father!" Too weak to throw off the attacker, his father calls upon Meir Katz, an old friend from his home town, who frees Eliezer. The father thus saves his son's life through a surrogate, one of the most robust in the group, but one who dies before the men reach Buchenwald and whose abandoned corpse is left on the train.

During the various phases of the nocturnal journey the other side of the rescue motif is also apparent: the son carefully watches over his father and at times delivers the latter from death. These brief moments of solidarity disrupt the machinery of destruction and prove to be examples of human resistance in the face of the inhuman. When Eliezer's father is selected for the gas chamber in Gleiwitz, the youth runs after him, creating enough confusion to finally reunite father and son in the right-hand column, this time the column of life. Shortly after this episode, Eliezer saves his father's life in the convoy to Buchenwald. Lying inert in the train, his father is taken for dead by the men who are throwing out the corpses. Eliezer desperately slaps his father's nearly lifeless face in an attempt to revive him and succeeds in making him move his eyelids slightly, a vital sign that he is still alive. The men leave him alone.

Upon arrival at the camp, the father reaches the breaking point. He sinks to the ground, resigned to dying. Eliezer is filled with rage at his father's passivity, and realizes he must now take charge. "I found my father weeping like a child," he says when later he finds him stretched across his bunk, crying bitterly after being beaten by the other inmates for not properly taking care of his bodily needs. The boy feeds his helpless father and brings him water. We see here the reversal of roles: the transformation of the once-powerful paternal authority into a weak, fearful child and that of the dependent child into an adult. By assuming responsibility for the sick old man, the son becomes a kind of father figure, illustrating Wiesel's contention that in the inverted world of the concentration camp, old men metamorphosed into children and children into old men in one never-ending night.

The reversal of roles in *Night* has been viewed by André Neher as "an anti-*Akeda:* not a father leading his son to be sacrificed, but a son guiding, dragging, carrying to the altar an old man who no longer has the strength to continue." Wiesel's text, he observes, is "a re-writing of the *Akeda* under the opaque light of Auschwitz. It is no longer a narrative invented by the imagination of a poet or philosopher. It is the reality of Auschwitz." This reality offers a sharp contrast to the biblical event. Whereas in the Bible God saves Isaac from being sacrificed by sending a ram to replace him, He does not intervene to save the father at the altar of Auschwitz. God allows the father to be consumed by Holocaust flames and the son is forced to recognize the inevitable—that he is impotent in the face of death's conquest and God's injustice. He must slowly watch his father acquiesce to death. Symbol of reason, strength, and humanity, the father finally collapses under the barbaric tactics of the Nazi oppressor to which Eliezer is a silent witness.

If the theme of father-son is characterized, in general, by the reciprocal support necessary for survival in extremity, the sanctity of the relationship is nevertheless violated by the camp conditions. In contrast to the son's need to protect and be protected by the father, there appears the opposing motif: the abandonment of the father. The Nazi technique of attempting to eradicate all family ties and creating a state of mind in which men view each other as enemies or strangers—what can be called the *concentration camp philosophy*—is demonstrated in *Night* through a series of incidents showing the competition for survival between fathers and sons.

Béla Katz, the son of a merchant from Eliezer's hometown and a member of the *Sonderkommando* in Birkenau, is forced to shove the body of his own father in to the crematory oven. A *pipel* in Buna beats his father because his father does not make his bed properly. A third instance, and the one the narrator constantly uses as a measure of his own behavior, is the deterioration of relations between Rabbi Eliahou and his son. Shunted from camp to camp for three years, the boy and his father have always managed to stay together. But after the seventy-kilometer march from Buna to Gleiwitz they are separated. The Rabbi reaches the shed and looks for his son. He tells Eliezer that in the obscurity of the night his son did not notice him fall to the rear of the column. However, Eliezer remembers seeing the youth run past the staggering old man and is horrified by this clear example of abandonment:

> A terrible thought loomed up in my mind: he had wanted to get rid of his father! He had felt that his father was growing weak, he had believed that the end was near and had sought this separation in order to get rid of the burden, to free himself from an encumbrance which could lessen his own chances of survival.

Eliezer prays to God to give him the strength never to do what Rabbi Eliahou's son has done.

Perhaps the most devastating example of the breakdown of human bonds occurs in the cattle cars going to Buchenwald during the final phase of the journey. Some workers amuse themselves by throwing pieces of bread into the open wagons and watching the starved men kill each other for a crumb.

Eliezer sees an old man about to eat a bit of break he was lucky enough to snatch from the crowd. Just as he brings the bread to his mouth, someone throws himself on top of him and beats him up. The old man cries out: "Meir, Meir, my boy! Don't you recognize me? I'm your father ... you're hurting me ... you're killing your father! I've got some bread ... for you too ... for you too ..." The son grabs the bread from his father's fist; the father collapses, murmurs something and then dies. As the son begins to devour the bread two men hurl themselves upon him and others join them. The young narrator is witness to the entire event: "When they withdrew, next to me were two corpses, side by side, the father and the son. I was fifteen years old."

Having witnessed fathers beaten, abandoned, and killed, the author, through his narrator, has chosen to represent the *son's betrayal of the father* and has omitted situations in which the father mistreats the son. ... By not being critical of the paternal figure in a world too often governed by viciousness, the author protects his father's image and honors his memory. This unconscious process of selection reveals the subjective aspect of the eyewitness account and of the survivor's perceptions. The focus upon the abuses of the sons is perhaps a projection of the author-narrator's own feeling of guilt; he identifies with them at the same time that he condemns them for having let their fathers perish. Despite Eliezer's efforts to save his father's life throughout the camp experience, the boy is critical of his own reprehensible behavior, and ultimately takes the blame for his father's death upon himself. ...

Yet more than the sense of complicity, after the father dies the son feels ambivalent and even somewhat liberated. Earlier in the text, his mixed emotions surface during an alert in Buchenwald, when Eliezer, separated from his father, does not bother to look for him. The next day he sets out but with highly conflicting feelings:

Don't let them find him! If only I could get rid of this dead weight, so that I could use all my strength to struggle for my own survival, and only worry about myself. Immediately I felt ashamed of myself, ashamed forever.

Eliezer's desire to rid himself of his oppressive burden, to lose his dependent father in the crowd, makes him recall with horror Rabbi Eliahou's son during the evacuation from Buna. When the narrator finally locates the feverish and trembling old man lying on a plank outside, he frantically claws his way through the crowd to get him some coffee. Later, he halfheartedly offers his dying father what is left of his own soup. While his deeds demonstrate care and devotion, his thoughts are of withdrawal and abandonment. Actions and intentionality, behavior and fantasies, do not correspond. The fifteen-year-old judges himself guilty: "No better than Rabbi Eliahou's son had I withstood the test." . . .

The ambivalent feelings of the fifteen-year-old with regard to his father and food are intensified after his father dies:

> I did not weep, and it pained me that I could not weep. But I had no more tears. And in the depths of my being, in the recesses of my weakened conscience, could I have searched it, I might perhaps have found something like— free at last.

The relief soon turns into a deep sense of guilt, for having failed to save his father, for having survived in his place, and for having thoughts of being liberated by his death. the protector has been transformed into a betrayer. Unconsciously, the youth may even feel that he has acted out a son's worst Oedipal fear: he has physically become "his father's murderer."

The survival guilt that Eliezer painfully endures culminates with the face in the mirror at the end of the narrative. . . .

The cadaverous reflection in the mirror also suggests the son's identification with the dead father, to whom he remains attached. According to Robert Jay Lifton, survival guilt is related to "the process of identification—the survivor's tendency to incorporate within himself an image of the dead, and then to think, feel and act as he imagines they would." At the end of the night, Eliezer incorporates his father into his own psyche and projects this image onto the mirror as his double. The haunting specter with its penetrating glance serves to keep the paternal presence alive and is the son's means of defending himself against his loss. The mirror image epitomizes Eliezer's state of mourning and his desire to join his father, whose death is experienced as a death of the self.

GARY HENRY ON TRANSCENDENCE IN WIESEL'S WORK

Elie Wiesel's literary work prompted one reviewer to recall Isaac Bashevis Singer's definition of Jews as "a people who can't sleep themselves and let nobody else sleep," and to predict, "While Elie Wiesel lives and writes, there will be no rest for the wicked, the uncaring or anyone else."[1] If uneasiness is the result of Wiesel's work, it is not a totally unintended result. Since the publication of *Night* in 1958, Wiesel, a Jewish survivor of the Nazi death camps, has borne a persistent, excruciating literary witness to the Holocaust. His works of fiction and non-fiction, his speeches and stories have each had the same intent: to hold the conscience of Jew and non-Jew (and, he would say, even the conscience of God) in a relentless focus on the horror of the Holocaust and to make this, the worst of all evils, impossible to forget.

Wiesel refuses to allow himself or his readers to forget the Holocaust because, as a survivor, he has assumed the role of messenger. It is his duty to witness as a "messenger of the dead among the living,"[2] and to prevent the evil of the victims' destruction from being increased by being forgotten. But he does not continue to retell the tales of the dead only to make life miserable for the living, or even to insure that such an atrocity will not happen again. Rather, Elie Wiesel is motivated by a need to wrestle theologically with the Holocaust.

The grim reality of the annihilation of six million Jews presents a seemingly insurmountable obstacle to further theological thought: how is it possible to believe in God after what happened? The sum of Wiesel's work is a passionate effort to break through this barrier to new understanding and faith. It is to his credit that he is unwilling to retreat into easy atheism, just as he refuses to bury his head in the sand of optimistic faith. What Wiesel calls for is a fierce, defiant struggle with the Holocaust, and his work tackles a harder question: how is it possible *not* to believe in God after what happened?[3]

It is not enough merely to value Wiesel for the poignancy of his experience and then summarily write him off as another "death of God" novelist. As bleak and nihilistic as some of his work may be, taken as a whole his writings are intensely theological. The death of God is not of more interest to Wiesel than the impossibility of God's death. And if this paradox is bewildering, it must be remembered that the Hasidism in which Wiesel's work is rooted is fascinated, rather than repelled by a paradox. Wiesel himself says, "As for God, I did speak about Him. I do little else in my books."[4] How Elie Wiesel speaks about God is the concern of this essay.

Wiesel and His Work

. . . Wiesel's own life as a boy was also something of a strange mixture. On the one hand, he gave himself fervently and almost completely to the Hasidic way of life. From early till late each day, ten or eleven months out of the year, he studied Torah, Talmud, and Kabbalah. He prayed and fasted and eagerly longed to penetrate the mysteries of Jewish mysticism, firmly settled in the conviction that he would be drawn "into eternity, into that time where question and answer become one."[6] His study and piety were of such intensity that he had little time for the usual joys of childhood and he became chronically weak and sickly from his habitual fasting.

Yet, both his mother and father urged him to combine modern secular studies with his devotion to Talmud and Kabbalah. Of his mother, he says, "Her dream was to make me into a doctor of philosophy; I should be both a Ph.D. and a rabbi."[7] And his father made him learn modern Hebrew, a skill with which he was later able to make his livelihood as a journalist for an Israeli newspaper. Wiesel remembers his father, an "emancipated," if religious Jew, saying to him, "Listen, if you want to study Talmud, if you want to study Kabbalah, whatever you want to study is all right with me and I'll help you. But you must give me one hour a day for modern study."[8] In that hour a day Wiesel digested books which his father brought him on psychology, astronomy, modern Hebrew literature, and music.

All of this study came to a halt in 1944 when, at the age of fifteen, Wiesel was deported with his family to the Nazi concentration camps at Auschwitz, Buna, and Buchenwald. There he and his father were separated from the mother and the girls. Early on, Wiesel's mother and youngest sister were killed by the Germans, and before the prisoners were liberated by the Allies, his father died of malnourishment and mistreatment.

After the liberation, Wiesel was sent to France along with four hundred other orphans. He spent two years as a ward of a French Jewish welfare agency, attempting to resume his religious studies. As the result of the publication of his photograph in a French newspaper, his two older sisters, who had survived the camps, were able to make contact with him. He had learned French and assumed French nationality by 1947 when he entered the Sorbonne. There he studied, among other things, philosophy and psychology. The Tel Aviv newspaper, *Yedioth Ahronoth*, hired him as a Paris correspondent, and because of the hard work of supporting himself as a journalist, he left the Sorbonne without submitting the six hundred-page doctoral dissertation he had written comparing Jewish, Christian, and Buddhist concepts of asceticism.

His journalistic work became his occupation and carried him to the Far East, to Palestine, and finally to New York in 1956. He was critically injured in an accident in New York and, unable to return to France, he became a U.S. citizen in 1963. He settled in New York and has lived there since with his wife, Marion, whom he married in 1968. Wiesel became a teacher in 1972 when he was invited to be Distinguished Professor of Jewish Studies at City College in New York. He filled that position until recently when he became Andrew Mellon Professor of Humanities at Boston University. . . .

Wiesel's literature is all of a piece with his life. His books, even the novels, are autobiographical. And each of them is a vital part of the mosaic formed by his past experiences, his spiritual growth, and his present activity. His books are far from being the products of some peripheral avocation, and still farther from being mere entertainment pieces. They mirror his own soul, and they were written in fulfillment of a mission which encompasses not only his writing, but everything else he does.

Since his books are so autobiographical and so intimately connected to one another and to his life, development is to be expected within Wiesel's work. Read in the order they were written, his books trace the torturous odyssey which has been his inner struggle to deal with the Holocaust. The early works are saturated with black despair, but by small degrees the successive pieces move toward Wiesel's triumphant achievement of faith in *Ani Maamin: A Song Lost and Found Again*. Even the titles of the early books suggest this progression: *Night, Dawn, Le Jour* (unfortunately entitled *The Accident* in the English edition).

Wiesel's first book, *Night*, is at the center of all he has written since. It is a somber, moving memoir of his faith-destroying experience in the death camps. Wiesel says of this book,

> *Night*, my first narrative, was an autobiographical story, a kind of testimony of one witness speaking of his own life, his own death. All kinds of options were available: suicide, madness, killing, political action, hate, friendship. I note all of these options: faith, rejection of faith, blasphemy, atheism, denial, rejection of man, despair and in each book I explore one aspect. In *Dawn* I explore the political action; in *The Accident*, suicide; in *The Town Beyond the Wall*, madness; in *The Gates of the Forest*, faith and friendship; in *A Beggar in Jerusalem*, history, the return. All the stories are one story except that I build them in concentric circles. The center is the same and is in *Night*.[9]

In addition to this successive exploration of possible responses to the Holocaust, there is another pattern to Wiesel's work: namely, the successive treatment in an entire book of one of the characters in *Night*.

Night was the foundation; all the rest is commentary. In each book, I take one character out of *Night* and give him a refuge, a book, a tale, a name, a destiny of his own.[10]

This structural center of Elie Wiesel's entire literary corpus comprises only 127 pages in its English paperback edition. When it was originally issued in Argentina in 1955, written in Yiddish, it ran to some 800 pages. The material cut out for the French edition in 1958 has provided the substance of much of Wiesel's subsequent "fiction"—so the novels are quite literally, as Wiesel says, commentary on *Night*.

Night, of course, stands for the Holocaust. The book poses the problem and depicts the abysmal blackness out of which Wiesel has struggled to free himself. In *Night* the young faith of the Hasid is devoured in the fires of the crematoria. God dies, and Wiesel's life is cursed. . .

Among other horrors, Wiesel and his fellow prisoners were forced to watch the hanging of a young boy by the Germans. The child was still alive when he filed past the scaffold and heard someone behind him wonder aloud, "Where is God? Where is He?"

And I heard a voice within me answer him: "Where is He? Here He is—He is hanging here on this gallows . . ." That night the soup tasted of corpses.[12]

It is a long distance between this bitter, raging despair and the eloquent hope expressed in Wiesel's cantata, *Ani Maamin*, . . . a defiant "I believe" *in spite* of what man has done and God has allowed to be done.

Story: The Witness as Writer

. . . Elie Wiesel is a witness, a teller of tales, and a writer, in that order. Each of these roles is determined by the Holocaust. As a survivor, Wiesel has no choice but to tell all who will listen what the silenced victims would tell if they could speak. He is a self-appointed witness in their behalf.

> I remember; during those years, when we were dreamless old children in a kingdom called Night, we had but one wish left but it was a burning desire: to bear witness.[14]

To that painful task of witness-bearing Wiesel is giving his life. His books, all of them, point to the Holocaust, and even the works of fiction are "not novels but pages of testimony."[15]

Wiesel has become the "spiritual archivist of the Holocaust"[16] for profound reasons. As we have seen, he believes he owes this work to the victims. Their dying wish was that at least one of their number might live to tell how they died—and Wiesel senses an awesome responsibility to testify for them. But also, he has said, "I write in order to understand as much as to be understood."[17] His testimony has been a means of coming to terms with the events themselves. And most fundamentally, he cherishes the hope that his witness may diminish the amount of suffering in the world. He can say bluntly of himself and other witnesses who carry the same burden, "We didn't write for any accepted purpose except for the extraordinary purpose of saving mankind."[18]

Wiesel's witness as survivor is twofold. There is a witness he must bear, certainly, to the non-Jew, the "executioner." But, as well, he must witness to the Jew, the "victim." In each case the testimony pricks the conscience.

> Mainly, my position in the Jewish community is really the position of a witness from within and a defender from without. This goes, of course, along with my ideas about the duties and the privileges of a storyteller—of a writer. From the inside, from within the community, I am critical. If Jews are criticized or attacked from the outside, then I try to defend them. What I try to do (it's very hard) is to reconcile the two attitudes: not to be too strong, too sharp, too critical when I am inside and not to be a liar on the outside.[19] . . .

But Wiesel is more than a bearer of testimony. He is an artist—a storyteller, a writer. True to his Hasidic roots, he believes in the power of the tale. . . .

In the Kabbalah, there is the story of *shvirat hakelim*, "the breaking of the vessels." This is the story of what went wrong at the Creation, the cosmic cataclysm. Wiesel says that his tale, and it is the same tale in one form or another, is of another cataclysm which took place a generation ago in the Holocaust. In a time when *this* tale can and must be told, all other stories become insignificant.

Wiesel's work renders the tale of the Holocaust into literary art. But because of the subject, the art is more than art. Since Auschwitz, literature can no longer be a mere diversion. The writer must write as witness.

> We are witnesses in the cruelest and strongest sense of the word. And we cannot stop. We must speak. This is what I am trying to do in my writing. I don't believe the aim of literature is to entertain, to distract, to amuse. It used to be. I don't believe in it anymore.[21]

When asked what it means to be a writer today, Wiesel has consistently said that it means to correct injustices, to alleviate suffering, to create hope. Precisely for this reason, the witness/storyteller/writer's work is disheartening. It so rarely accomplishes what it must accomplish.

> All this will tell you why a person of my time who has to be a witness for himself (and I try to do it in my writing as much as I can), literally feels despair. I think that never before has Judaism reached such a spiritual low. There is no idealism anymore. There is no awareness.[22]

Wiesel's role as witness so thoroughly governs his role as writer that he must continue to write whether his testimony meets with any response or not.

> One must write out of one's own experience, out of one's own identity. One must cater to no one; one must remain truthful. If one is read, it's good; if one is not read, it's too bad. But that should not influence the writer.[23]

And, most important, the witness' work as writer demands that he write as a moral man. The literary artist can no longer be excused if he writes one way and lives another. Life and story must blend in ethical harmony. The writer is bound in a moral commitment by the very tale he tells. The making and reading of literature is no frivolous business.

> True writers want to tell the story simply because they believe they can do something with it—their lives are not fruitless and are not spent in vain. True listeners want to listen to stories to enrich their own lives and to understand them. What is happening to me happens to you. Both the listener and the reader are participants in the same story and both *make* it the story it is. I speak only of true writers and true readers and true listeners. As for the others, they are entertainers and their work doesn't really matter. I don't want to go into names but there are very few great storytellers and great writers today. Actually, I believe that today literature has changed its purpose and its dimension. Once upon a time it was possible to write *l'art pour l'art*, art for art's sake. People were looking only for beauty. Now we know that beauty without an ethical dimension cannot exist. We have seen what they did with culture in Germany during the war; what they called culture did not have any ethical purpose or motivation. I believe in the ethical thrust, in the ethical function, in the human adventure in science or in culture or in writing.[24]

The witness begins with his testimony. In Wiesel's case this testimony concerns the Holocaust. He becomes a true writer when his testimony is a tale, a story. The art of the witness, then, is a rendering of testimony into story. The difficulty of this lies in the attempt to juxtapose past event with present situation in a story which is truly artistic: that is, not merely beautiful, but ethically significant. Wiesel is cut off from the victims whose tale he tells (he survived), and he is cut off from his readers (they have not seen what he has seen). The monumental task which Wiesel has attempted has been to bring together in his tales the disparate worlds of the Holocaust victims in the past and of his post-Holocaust readers in the present. Wiesel lives in both worlds, yet hardly belongs to either. His effort has been to force into an imaginative form, a story, these disjunctive worlds. The result has been something of a literary anomaly: "autobiographical" novels.

The survivor's alienation from both past and present and its implications for the witness as writer are best seen in Wiesel's use of the concept of "madness." The witness as writer is in the position of Moshe the Beadle in *Night*. Able to return to Sighet as a survivor from an early deportation, Moshe was disbelieved and considered mad when he tried to tell the tale of those who did *not* escape. Moshe the Madman appears in nearly all of Wiesel's work, and he even becomes the main character in one novel, *The Oath*. As a "messenger of the dead among the living," who attempts with his tales to save the living but is regarded as insane, Moshe is a paradigm for Wiesel of the madman as witness.

Wiesel is qualified to speak of madness. During his three years at the Sorbonne, he specialized in clinical psychology, and the New York Society of Clinical Psychologists has honored him for his perceptive treatment of madness in his writing.[25] This work, his concentration camp experiences, and his Hasidic background unite to make madness one of the leading motifs in his books.

According to Wiesel, there are several kinds of madness. First, there is clinical insanity. Wiesel cautions, however, that what is often considered madness in this sense may not be insanity at all, but merely dissent from the "collective neurosis" of society. In a society gone "mad," the sane person will be judged mad, even though it is society and not he that suffers from skewed vision. Just as a sane inmate in an insane asylum would be judged mad by the other inmates, so anyone whose vision is threatening or disturbing to "normal" society is considered mad. . . .

This madness of the witness is a "prophetic" madness. It is the madness of an individual who has seen things inaccessible to others, and is therefore separated from other men by the very fact of his closeness to God. Wiesel views this type of madman as a messenger of God and says, "God loves madmen. They're the only ones he allows near him."[27] The strangeness of his tale renders the prophet an anti-social misfit, a madman, in the eyes of his contemporaries. Thus, prophecy has long been considered a species of madness.[28] Like Wiesel, the Holocaust survivor, the prophetic madman is a lonely figure, separated from the world by the witness he bears and yet compelled to live in the world as a man among men.

There is still another type of madness: moral madness. Thomas Merton has written that "the whole concept of sanity in a society where spiritual values have lost their meaning is itself meaningless."[29] When hate and indifference are the norm in society, one must become morally mad to protest against society's inhumanity. In the Germany of 1943, one had to choose moral madness to avoid being swallowed up by the prevailing "sanity." In such a context, moral indifference is the type of insanity against which moral madness must protest. This moral madness, a voluntary, deliberate thing,[30] is no easy "out" or surrender. It is a courageous identification with the sufferers, a true loving and caring. It is the willing assumption of moral responsibility in a society whose conscience is asleep. Not to accept moral madness is to opt for true insanity. Wiesel says,

> I believe that reality disappointed us so much that I seek something in another reality. So what is the other reality? Madness. I believe that anyone who was in the camps came out deranged. There is the basis of madness in every person who survived. When you have seen what they have seen, how can you not keep some madness? This in itself would be mad—to remain normal.[31]

Notes

1. Mayo Mohs, "Jeremiah II," review of A Jew Today, by Elie Wiesel, in *Time*, December 25, 1978, p. 81.

2. *The Accident* (New York: Hill and Wang, 1962), p. 45.

3. *The Gates of the Forest* (New York: Holt, Rinehart and Winston, 1966), p. 194.

4. "Jewish Values in the Post-Holocaust Future: A Symposium," *Judaism* (Summer, 1967), p. 298.

6. *Night* (New York: Avon, 1960), p. 14.

7. Harry James Cargas, *In Conversation with Elie Wiesel*, p. 73.

8. *Ibid.*, pp. 75-76.

9. *Ibid.*, p. 86.

10. *Ibid.*, p. 3.

12. *Ibid.*, p. 76.

14. "To Remain Human in Face of Inhumanity," condensed from an address, *The Jewish Digest*, XVII (September, 1972), p. 40.

15. *Ibid.*

16. Curt Leviant, "Elie Wiesel: A Soul on Fire," *Saturday Review*, January 31, 1970, p. 25.

17. David Greenstein, "On Elie Wiesel," *Jewish Frontier*, October, 1974, p. 19.

18. Harry James Cargas, *In Conversation with Elie Wiesel*, p. 4.

19. *Ibid.*, p. 33.

21. Morton A. Reichek, "Elie Wiesel: Out of the Night," p. 45.

22. "Words from a Witness," condensed from an address, *Conservative Judaism*, XXI (Spring, 1967), p. 44.

23. Harry James Cargas, *In Conversation with Elie Wiesel*, p. 34.

24. *Ibid.*, pp.86-87.

25. Morton A. Reichek, "Elie Wiesel: Out of the Night," pp. 42, 43.

27. *The Town Beyond the Wall* (New York: Holt, Rinehart and Winston,1964), p. 19.

28. Plato writes in the *Phaedrus* (244), "There is also a madness which is a divine gift and the source of the chiefest blessings granted to men. For prophecy is a madness." Jewish prophets in the biblical period were often considered mad by the citizenry: "The prophet is a fool; the man of spirit is mad" (Hosea 9:7).

29. Thomas Merton, *Raids on the Unspeakable* (New York: New Directions, 1966), p. 47.

30. Wiesel quotes Dostoevski at the beginning of *The Town Beyond the Wall*: "I have a plan—to go mad."

31. Morton A. Reichek, "Elie Wiesel: Out of the Night," p. 43.

Try to imagine the ideological gap that exists between those who struggle to find meaning in the Holocaust and those who deny its reality. . . . On the one side we find survivors, clergy, scholars, and the simply concerned engaged, whether they realize it or not, in a theology of destruction, taking measure of a darkness so vast it nearly looks like God. On the other we have the likes of David Irving, Michael Hoffman, Robert Faurisson—the kind of historians-on-the-side who assert that Zyklon B was merely a pesticide, that the number of Jews murdered was actually far less than is contended, that anyway they died of typhus, and that, really, nothing much happened at all.

"These are morally sick individuals," Nobel Prize winner Elie Wiesel has said of revisionists. "While I am able to fight against injustice, I have no idea how to go about fighting against ugliness." For their part, Faurisson and company refer to Wiesel—a man the *Washington Post* once referred to as "a symbol, a banner, a beacon, perhaps the survivor of the Holocaust"—as the "Prominent False Witness," and, when good old-fashioned name-calling will do, "Elie Weasel." . . .

[W]hat is theology if not a kind of revisionism? In the landscape of human discourse, theology occupies the place between fiction and history, myth and memory. It is from this place that Wiesel has said, "Auschwitz is as important as Sinai." Insofar as the Holocaust has changed humanity's relationship with God every bit as much as the giving of the Law, there is no denying that this is true. . . . While he considers different responses to this Event in each of his books, throughout his work Wiesel treats the Holocaust first of all as a theological occurrence. As with God's word at Mount Sinai, as with God's test at Mount Moriah, the occasion of God's greatest silence exists for Wiesel outside of time. It is an Event of such magnitude it transcends history.

Transcending history, though, is a tricky business. Sinai need not be historical for it to have meaning. If Auschwitz is granted the same status, is it not at risk of sharing this implication? In making the Holocaust primarily a matter of theological concern, does Elie Wiesel, witness to the world, court a benign sort of revisionism? At a time when it has become commonplace for revisionists to snarl that the Holocaust is a religion and Wiesel its prophet, what are we to do with a theological Auschwitz? . . .

"That the extermination of the Jews of Europe ought to arrest the attention of theologians seems obvious," the historian Amos Funkenstein once wrote. . . . [He] has identified three distinct varieties of theological response to the Holocaust. . . .

The first he names is the direct theological response: it is the attempt "to salvage a theodicy from the rubble left by the eruption of evil as an apparently autonomous force." On the one hand this may mean religious Zionism: the phoenix Israel born of Diaspora's ashes. On the other, it is the rarely voiced haredim we-told-you-so: European Jewry did not die because they were Jews, but rather because they had forgotten they were Jews. With the Holocaust, in other words, God reopened the floodgates. . . .

Elie Wiesel's Holocaust theology does not fit neatly into any of Funkenstein's categories. This is not surprising, as the exact nature of his theology has been seldom addressed. Theological critique often becomes a kind of blasphemy, and this is especially true in the case of a doubly sacred survivor-theologian like Wiesel. While his religious voice remains much discussed, it is little dissected. For fear of the implications of approaching a witness critically, few have been willing even to make the attempt.

One who has is Naomi Seidman, a professor of Jewish Culture at the Graduate Theological Union in Berkeley, California. She tried recently to find answers to questions raised by Wiesel's theological understanding through textual analysis, and in the process learned first hand the hazards of Holocaust theology.

In the last months of 1996, the young Yiddish literary scholar published a paper greeted by some as heresy, by others as the long-awaited slaying of a sacred cow. By comparing Wiesel's *Night* to its earlier draft, *Un di velt hot geshvign* ("And the world remained silent") published in Yiddish in 1956, Seidman undertook the first genuine criticism of the much revered book, shedding light on its journey from a bare-bones accounting of events to the existentialist memoir that for many has come to typify the Holocaust. What she documented, essentially, is Wiesel's growth—his translation, perhaps—from survivor/witness to writer/theologian.

Using a method akin to biblical source criticism, Seidman's paper traced the text's development layer by layer, and predictably ruffled fundamentalist feathers. Letters written in response to the paper declared it a "futile and ugly performance." Critics railed its author as "ill-informed," incompetent in the language of her scholarship, and worse: "Ms. Seidman's brand of Holocaust revisionism is more deadly than Holocaust denial," one of the letters said, "it is a corrosive poison that destroys from within." Even to research Holocaust theology, apparently, is to court revisionism—or, at least, to appear to do so.

Writing in Seidman's defense, Steven Zipperstein, the editor of *Jewish Social Studies*, ... wrote, the attack on Seidman "conflates Mr. Wiesel with the Holocaust itself in its contention that his work cannot be interpreted critically without resorting to Holocaust revisionism."

Elsewhere Seidman was lionized as "foremost among our younger generation of scholars," and, with such support, ultimately she won the day. Rightly so: original, challenging, and crucial to reaching an understanding of Wiesel and the development of his thought, Seidman's paper is a careful and important piece of work....

Employed at the time by a Jewish cultural organization, moving in Yiddishist and Judaic Studies circles, I had heard about the paper and its mixed reception when it first was published. Yet I did not read it until recently. While trying to track down a copy of *Un di velt hot geshvign*, I remembered

Professor Seidman had done work with it, and so did a web search on her name. Along with her homepage at GTU, up popped a link in blue letters: "Elie Wiesel and the Scandal of Jewish Rage."

Pleased as I was to stumble across the storied essay, I was puzzled that the link was not to the website of *Jewish Social Studies*, but to that of a group called AAARGH: *L'Association des Anciens Amateurs de Recits de Guerre et d'Holocauste*. My French is far from fluent; it took me a few minutes to realize exactly what I had found.

From AAARGH's introduction:

This article describes the first phases of the formation of one of the great impostors of our time. . . . Holocaust literature is the largest construction of our era, and Wiesel is its prophet.

Having survived one round of controversy, Naomi Seidman's careful, important piece of work happened upon another. It had found new life in a forum devoted to denying the Holocaust. It was an intellectual hijacking that had as much to do with her subject as her findings.

As its title suggests, "Elie Wiesel and the Scandal of Jewish Rage" is concerned with anger, more specifically with the consideration of vengefulness as a common, appropriate and yet rarely acknowledged response to Jewish suffering. It deals also, however, with the historical development of Wiesel's theology.

Finding *Night* lacking "Jewish rage" in sufficient quantity in relation to both the circumstances which inspired it and the Yiddish text from which it was born, Seidman alleges that Wiesel excised all traces of the survivor's desire for retribution when *Un di velt hot geshvign* became *Night*. In a news item which sparked much of the controversy of the paper's initial publication, the *Jewish Daily Forward* reported, "In editing his Yiddish memoir for his French publisher, Ms. Seidman told the *Forward* by telephone from her Berkeley office, Mr. Wiesel 'replaced an angry survivor desperate to get his story out, eager to get revenge and who sees life, writing, testimony as a refutation of what the Nazis did to the Jews, with a survivor haunted by death, whose primary complaint is directed against God, not the world, [or] the Nazis.'"

Building a case that the two memoirs tell significantly different stories, Seidman provides cogent examples of curious choices Wiesel made when reworking the original into French. Some of these are arguably matters of perception. In the first book, for example, the Wiesel family's home, Sighet, is referred to as a *shtot*, a city, while in the second it is "that little town . . . where I spent my childhood"—essentially the archetypal shtetl. Such a change could easily be accounted for by nostalgia, or by the fact that by the time the second book was written the author, working as he did between one book and the next as a foreign correspondent, had seen far more of the world. . . .

In other instances, however, the differences are such that it is hard not to see an agenda. When describing the post-emancipation activities of some of the camp survivors, for example, Wiesel reports some of the boys run off, in Yiddish, "*tsu fargvaldikn daytshe shikses*," while in French they merely go "*coucher avec des filles . . .*"

"To sleep with young girls," as the French has it, is hardly an adequate translation of the Yiddish, "to rape German shikses." Obviously, it is an entirely different telling of the event. "There are two survivors," Seidman writes, "a Yiddish and a French"—and two survivors will of course tell different stories.

Seidman's contention is that far from being mere matters of word choice, episodes like the one involving *fargvaldikn* and *coucher avec* suggest that the latter book is not merely a translated and edited edition, but rather an entirely different book written for an entirely different audience for entirely different reasons.

Well aware of the implications of this claim, and perhaps back-peddling in the face of the assault she received, Seidman elaborated in a letter to the *Forward*: "To speak differently when you speak in a differently language, is neither hypocritical nor inauthentic; it is merely human, rarely deliberate, and perhaps inevitable."

The editors of AAARGH apparently disregarded this clarification. Already they had found enough damning material to warrant conscripting Seidman's words to their cause.

Because *Night* is not, as the paper shows, the unmediated experience its more naive readers may suppose it to be, it is for the revisionists entirely false, a lie upon which larger lies have been built. Thus the revisionists' ostensible reason for republishing "Elie Wiesel and the Scandal of Jewish Rage" is the implication, as they read it, that its subject, their nemesis, is a fraud.

Not surprisingly, this is a surface take on Seidman's reading of Wiesel. The import of ". . . the Scandal of Jewish Rage" is found not in the factual discrepancy between a book and its rewrite, nor in the headline grabbing contentions that Wiesel clothed such crimes as rape in the stubborn vitality of the Jewish people. Neither is the heart of the paper Wiesel's supposed suppression of further incidents of Jewish retribution.

Rather the real story here is of the development of Wiesel's theology. The differences between the Yiddish telling and the French can be accounted for by this theology, as can revisionist interest in Seidman's work. So too, in fact, can the endless revisionist obsession with Wiesel himself.

"Let me be clear," Seidman writes. "The interpretation of the Holocaust as a religious theological event is not a tendentious imposition on *Night* but rather a careful reading of the work." That this is true can best be seen when *Night* is set against *Un di velt*, of which the same could not be said.

According to Seidman, Wiesel's first book should be considered as part of the larger genre of Yiddish Holocaust memoirs, which "often modeled themselves on the local chronicle (*pinkes*) or memorial book (*yizker-bukh*) in which catalogs of names, addresses, and occupations served as form and motivation."

Though it is largely a work of history, however, the earlier book does allow God his place. One letter writer to the *Forward* was right to insist, "Not only are all the French version's famous passages about God present in the Yiddish volume, but the latter contains other equally harrowing examples of the young death camp inmate's struggle with his faith."

In fact, God's role in *Un di velt* is not entirely unlike that in *Night*. In both God is wholly and substantially absent. In the Yiddish, though, this is a different sort of absence. It is the immediate, obvious absence faced by the victim rather than the reflective, philosophical absence later experienced by the survivor. It is the difference between an absence felt by a man under duress and one who is trying to rebuild his life.

As Wiesel tells it in his memoir, *All Rivers Run to the Sea*, *Un di velt hot geshvign* was written years after liberation, while en route to Argentina. "I spent most of the voyage in my cabin working. I was writing my account of the concentration camp years—in Yiddish. I wrote feverishly, breathlessly, without rereading. I wrote to testify, to stop the dead from dying, to justify my own survival."

Yet as he explains in the final pages of the book itself—written earlier, closer to the event and so perhaps more reliably—the composition of *Un di velt* actually began far sooner, sooner even than seems imaginable. *Night* reads: "Three days after the Liberation of Buchenwald I became very ill with food poisoning. I was transferred to the hospital and spent two weeks between life and death." *Un di velt* continues: "I stayed in bed for a few more days, in the course of which I wrote the outline of the book you are holding in your hand, dear reader. . ." Thus Wiesel's telling of the story began even before he had lived its end. In fact, he began telling the story before he knew he would live at all: "So I thought it would be a good idea to publish a book based on the notes I wrote in Buchenwald."

Taking the book at its word, it seems possible that something like a rough draft of *Un di velt hot geshvign* was written, or at least considered, even while Wiesel remained in the camps. It's no surprise, then, that unlike *Night*, it is difficult to read the earlier book as theology. At times, in fact, it reads as a clear rebuke of the religious response to suffering.

The most telling scene in this regard did not have problems of translation moving from Yiddish to French—because it does not appear in *Night* at all.

The opening lines of *Un di velt hot geshvign* are missing not only from *Night* but, strangely, from Seidman's comparison of the works.

Un di velt hot geshvign begins "*in onheyb,*" "in the beginning," as do most Yiddish translations of Genesis and the Gospel of John. By the time he put pen to paper, perhaps making notes in Buchenwald, Wiesel certainly would have read the former, and, a curious young man, a budding intellectual, very likely the latter. Beginning as he does, Wiesel leans in close to scripture, unafraid to show his resemblance to it. He nods graciously to his influences, and then he spits on them:

> In the beginning was belief, foolish belief, and faith, empty faith, and illusion, the terrible illusion. . . . We believed in God, had faith in man, and lived with the illusion that in each one of us is a holy spark from the fire of the shekinah, that each one carried in his eyes and in his soul the sign of God. This was the source—if not the cause—of all our misfortune.

These are Wiesel's first published words, and there is no indictment like it in anything he has written since. In the form of this past-tense creed—not "we believe," but "we believed"—the young Wiesel refutes religion as a whole; in its content, he refutes Judaism particularly; in its details, Kabbalah, Jewish mysticism, a mainstay of his later work, specifically. Belief is foolish, faith is empty, the in-dwelling God is a fantasy long purchased but still not worth the price. This is Wiesel's theology as seen through the dark lens of *Un di velt hot geshvign.*

What becomes of this in *Night?* . . . [I]t disappears.

Night's beginning, "They called him Moche the Beadle," can be found several pages into *Un di velt.* Wiesel has stated that the only real difference between the books is the length; that he "shortened, shortened, shortened" the manuscript for purposes of concision. Looking at one beginning and the other, however, it is clear that there were also theological considerations at work. The original opening has in effect been replaced by

French Catholic intellectual François Mauriac's problematic christological introduction:

> And I [Mauriac], who believes that God is love, what answer could I give my young questioner [Wiesel], whose dark eyes still held the reflection of that angelic sadness which had appeared one day upon the face of the hanged child? What did I say to him? Did I speak of that other Jew, his brother, who may have resembled him—the Crucified, whose Cross has conquered the world?

The very religious principles made to bear the weight of Wiesel's scorn in *Un di velt . . .* are in *Night* enshrined in a narrative of a holy Jewish childhood. "I believed profoundly," Wiesel writes. "During the day I studied the Talmud, and at night I ran to the synagogue to weep over the destruction of the Temple." There is no mention anywhere in *Night* that Jewish belief was the cause of Jewish misfortune. Thus faith is pulled from the rubble. Also patched and salvaged from the wreck of *Un di velt* is Kabbalah, which in *Night* is not maligned but rather sought out as the height of knowledge. Another sentence not to be found in Yiddish: "One day I asked my father to find me a master to guide me in my studies of the cabbala."

What was regarded as illusion in one book becomes deepest truth in another. Why? Wiesel was kind enough to provide a possible explanation: "Maimonides said it was only at thirty that one had the right to venture into the perilous world of mysticism. You must first pass the basic subjects within your own understanding." And that seems precisely what Wiesel, at thirty, did in rewriting his first book. Having exhausted his historical understanding of events in *Un di velt hot geshvign* he moved on to mystery with *Night*.

As *Night* makes clear, Wiesel's unique brand of mysticism is crucial to understanding his theology. The key to both can be found in the figure of Moche the Beadle, and in the differences, again, between this character and his Yiddish counterpart. For purposes of clarity while discussing these differences, I'll refer to the Beadle (or *Shamas*) of *Un di velt* as Moshele, as he is called in Yiddish, and that of *Night* as Moche.

In the Yiddish, Moshele has just one role in the narrative. He is introduced immediately as one who had come back, "from there! from there" That is, he is one who has been where the truth of the Holocaust is well known. He reports what he knows and has seen to the Jews of Sighet and they, to his dismay, do not believe him.

Moche serves this purpose also in *Night*. Returning to Sighet months after deportation, he is found sitting by the synagogue door:

> He told his story and that of his companions. The Jews . . . were made to dig huge graves, And when they had finished their work, the Gestapo began theirs. Without passion, without haste, they slaughtered their prisoners. Each one had to go up to the hole and present his neck. Babies were thrown into the air and the machine gunners used them as targets. This was in the forest of Galicia, near Kolomaye. How had Moche the Beadle escaped? Miraculously . . .

In each book the Beadle serves as first witness. Like Wiesel himself, Moche and Moshele are privy to awful truths the world does not want to hear. This, it must be stressed, is Moshele's only function in *Un di velt hot geshvign*. To put it bluntly: he is introduced, he testifies, he is doubted and then, of course, proven correct.

In *Night*, however, Moche serves a more complex narrative and theological purpose. Taking on another and equally important role, it is he who initiates Eliezer into the mysteries of Kabbalah. The following does not appear in the original book: "He had noticed me one day at dusk, while I was praying. . . . 'Why do you pray?' he asked me, after a moment. Why do I pray? A strange question. Why do I live? Why do I breath? . . . After that day I saw him often. He explained to me with great insistence that every question possessed a power that did not lie in the answer."

That nearly every word in *Night* regarding Kabbalah and other of the more esoteric aspects of Judaism has been added to a text that was supposedly "shortened, shortened, shortened" suggests that the most striking and intentional difference between the Yiddish and the French is not the suppression of Jewish rage, as Seidman contends, but rather the imposition of a theological frame on the story.

Just as there are two survivors responsible for the presentation of Wiesel's story, there are two witnesses within it. One is historical, Moshele; the other is theological, Moche. In the translation of Moshele, who is only witness, into Moche, who is witness and sage, Wiesel has created a mouthpiece for his theology. It is a unique Holocaust theology, a theology of questions without answers; one that equates knowledge of the depths of man's depravity with knowledge of the heights of man's wisdom. Moche is Master of both, and through him Wiesel the writer gives voice to Wiesel the theologian:

> "Man raises himself toward God by the question he asks Him," he was fond of repeating. "That is the true dialogue. Man questions God and God answers. But we don't understand His answers. We can't understand them. Because they come from the depths of the soul, and they stay there until death. You will find the true answers only within yourself."
>
> "There are a thousand and one gates leading into the orchard of mystical truth. Every human being has his own gate. We must never make the mistake of wanting to enter the orchard by any gate but our own . . ."

To speak of questions and gates here is portentous, foreshadowing the gates of the camps and the questions to God the camps will raise. Already we begin to see the theologizing of the Event. In *Night* the teacher of the mystical secrets becomes also the teacher of the truth of the camps. Who is to say whether it was the theologian or the writer in Wiesel who could not resist the symmetry of it? Regardless, this development marks the birth of the theology that informs all of

Wiesel's work. Through Moche, Auschwitz for Wiesel comes to stand for the mystery of darkness, Kabbalah, the mystery of light. To create such a schema, though, is to fit the Holocaust into a rather tidy cosmology. Whatever this says for the skills and imagination of a writer, it does little service to history.

Joseph Sungolowsky on Holocaust Autobiography

No matter how truthful the autobiographer tries to be, he cannot avoid having recourse to fictional or literary devices. Indeed, autobiography is necessarily linked to related literary genres such as the novel, the theater, the diary, or the chronicle.[36] Thus, despite Theodor W. Adorno's contention that it is barbaric to write literature after Auschwitz, the Holocaust writer or autobiographer must engage in a "writing experience" if he wishes to express himself.

The terse language of Wiesel's *Night* is occasionally broken by harrowing scenes such as that of Madame Shachter gone mad in the cattle car or by dialogues such as those that take place between himself and his erstwhile master Moshe-the-Beadle or with his dying father. Fantasy is present when he depicts his native Sighet as "an open tomb" after its Jews have been rounded up. He uses irony when he recalls that a fellow inmate has faith in Hitler because he has kept all his promises to the Jewish people. Images express the author's feelings. Gallows set up in the assembly place in preparation of a hanging appear to him as "three black crows," and the violin of a fellow inmate who has died after playing a Beethoven concerto lies beside him like "a strange overwhelming little corpse." The grotesque best portrays his fellow inmates, "Poor mountebanks, wider than they were tall, more dead than alive; poor clowns, their ghostlike faces emerging from piles of prison clothes! Buffoons!"[37] . . .

As painful as it may be to both author and reader, these autobiographical writings attempt to come to grips with the hard reality of the concentrationary universe. If *Night* has become a classic, it is because it remains one of the most concise and factual eyewitness accounts of the horrors. Wiesel goes into such details as the early disbelief of the victims ("The yellow star? Oh! well, what of it?" says his own father), the anguish of those who have been marked by death by Mengele in the course of a selection and Wiesel's own joy at having escaped it, the careless trampling of inmates by their own comrades in the course of the agonizing death marches. . . .

"Autobiography," writes George May, "is capable of absorbing the most diverse material, to assimilate it and to change it into autobiography."[51] Inasmuch as Holocaust autobiography deals with the events of one of the greatest upheavals of the twentieth century and the most traumatic destruction of the Jewish people, it is natural that autobiographers reflect upon the impact of those events on their personality, on the destiny of the Jewish people and on the post-Holocaust world.

Confession is an essential ingredient of autobiography. Its degree of sincerity remains the sole prerogative of the autobiographer who can choose to shield himself behind his own writing. In Wiesel's *Night*, the frankness of his confession serves as a testimony to the extent of the dehumanization he has reached as a result of his concentration-camp life. While he has been separated forever from his mother and sister upon arrival in Auschwitz, he has managed to stay with his father. Both have miraculously escaped selection for death on several occasions. Yet, the survival instinct has overtaken him in the face of his dying father. When a guard tells him that in the camp "there are no fathers, no brothers, no friends," he thinks in his innermost heart that the guard is right but does not dare admit it. When he wakes up the next morning (less than four months before the Liberation) to find his father dead, he thinks "something like—free at last."[52] Henceforth, Wiesel's life is devoid of meaning. *Night* concludes with the episode of the author looking at himself in the mirror. He writes: "a corpse gazed at me. The look in his eyes as they stared into mine has never left me."[53] As indicated by Ellen Fine, the shift from the first to the third person in that sentence points to the "fragmented self,"[54] and, as indicated by Wiesel himself, that sight was to determine his career as a "writer-witness."[55] . . .

The Holocaust causes [Wiesel] to question God's ways. One of the main themes of *Night* is Wiesel's shattered faith. When he recalls his arrival in Auschwitz, he writes the now famous words: "Never shall I forget those flames which consumed my faith forever."[60] He subsequently doubts God's justice,[61] argues with God on Rosh-Hashanah,[62] eats on Yom Kippur as an act of defiance against God, and feels that God Himself is hanging on the gallows when he witnesses the hanging of a child.[63] In fact, the "Trial of God"[64] obsesses Wiesel throughout the work.

Notes

36. Philippe Lejeune, *L'Autobiographie en France*. Paris: Armand Colin, 1971, p. 28; Georges May, *L'Autobiographie*. Paris: Presses Universitaires de France, 1979, pp. 113–116.

37. Elie Wiesel, *Night*. New York: Avon Books, 1969, p. 94. For a literary evaluation of *Night*, see Lawrence L. Langer, *The Holocaust and the Literary Imagination*. New Haven & London: Yale University Press, 1975, pp. 75–89; Ted L. Estess, *Elie Wiesel*, pp. 17–32.

51. May, pp. 200–201.

52. Wiesel, *Night*, pp. 122–124. For a thorough and moving analysis of the father-son relationship in *Night*, see Ellen S. Fine, *Legacy of Night: The Literary Universe of Elie Wiesel*. Albany: State University Press, 1982, pp. 18–26.

53. Wiesel, *Night*, p. 127.

54. Fine, p. 25.

55. *Harry James Cargas in Conversation with Elie Wiesel*. New York: Paulist Press, 1976, p. 88.

60. Wiesel, *Night*, p. 44.

61. *Ibid.*, p. 55.

62. *Ibid.*, p. 79

63. *Ibid.*, p. 76.

64. Such is indeed the title of one of Wiesel's plays.

SABINE AND HARRY STEIN ON THE HISTORY OF BUCHENWALD

Construction Period

The first concentration camps in Germany were built after the mass arrests which accompanied Hitler's seizure of power in 1933. While these camps did not last for a long time in many cases, the number of new and large camps started to rise continuously during the second half of the 1930s. They formed a network which covered Germany and was extended subsequently to every occupied country. The names of these camps became synonymous with traumatic experience such as hunger, cold, torture and the murder of millions of men, women and children.

The concentration camp on Ettersberg Hill near Weimar was founded in 1937. Its first name was "Ettersberg Concentration Camp". The decision to select this site was made because it was close to Weimar, the capital of Thuringia, because of its proximity to exploitable clay and stone deposits and finally, because Sauckel, the regional chief of the Nazi party, wanted to have a large contingent of SS troops stationed near Weimar. The hill and its lush forests situated north of the town used to be a popular place for excursions made by Weimar's inhabitants since Goethe's time. In due course, however, the cultural community of National Socialists in Weimar found it unacceptable to give the name of a place associated with Goethe to this camp. Whereas the town of classical German literature had become a place of worship for the National Socialists, the name of Buchenwald, a place just 8 kilometres from Weimar, was to become infamously engraved upon the world's memory.

The SS pressed ahead with the establishment of the camp showing mercy neither to man nor to nature. The workforce comprised 149 men at the beginning, more than 1000 in August 1937 and more than 2500 men at the turn of the year from 1937 to 1938. They all had to toil until late at night to develop the site and build SS barracks, houses for the commanders and their own miserable quarters. At the beginning, the prison community consisted of political opponents to National Socialism, of recidivists (or habitual criminals) and Jehovah's Witnesses.

Several thousand men joined the camp community in 1938. They included persistent offenders, vagrants, so-called social misfits and homosexuals. In 1938, the Gestapo took more than 13,000 Jews from Germany and Austria to this camp. They were arrested early in the summer and autumn and also after the anti-Jewish pogroms in November. Hundreds of Sinti Gypsies were among the prisoners arrested in 1938.

People put into the camp lost everything which had individuated their personalities as well as their appearance thus far. Their hair was shaved off, they were given numbers and divided into certain categories distinguishable by triangles of different coloured fabric. Their names, professions and social status were subject to systematic devaluation. The aim of camp detention was to wipe out all individual differences and aspirations. Hannah Arendt later wrote that concentration camps were "laboratories to find out by experiment whether the fundamental claim of totalitarian regimes was true and whether complete control could be exerted over humans". The methods of torture used in these laboratories included hunger, beating and murder and they produced a type of murderer hitherto unknown in the history of modern civilization, who killed people in a calculating, cold and systematic way. Death was ubiquitous. "To die was the prisoner's last duty", writes Jean Améry, a survivor of Auschwitz and Buchenwald. The first in a long series of victims was the worker Hermann Kempeck murdered at the age of 23 on the 13th August 1938.

Dirty and narrow accommodation, lack of sanitary facilities, urgent need of water and long working hours of up to 14 to 16 hours marked the lives of prisoners from the first day on. The harsh climate on the northern slope of the Ettersberg and the insufficient clothing of the prisoners led to many cases of frostbite occurring mainly during work outside in winter and often resulting in the amputation of limbs. The camp was crammed with people from time to time. This happened for instance in the second half of 1938. Many people and especially Jews were packed into provisional accommodation.

Right from the outset, the individual prisoners and the various groups of prisoners had varying statuses within the prison hierarchy of the camp determined mainly by the SS. Essential camp services had to be run largely by the prisoners themselves. A bitter struggle started between the "Politicals" and the "Criminals" because this work promised influence and a better social status.

The internal hierarchy in the camp also determined the chances of survival. Jews, Sinti and Romany Gypsies, homosexuals and later on Soviet prisoners of war lived in permanent danger of being killed. The SS established a terrorist regime under the Camp Commandant Karl Koch. It included roll calls to count the prisoners in the morning and at night, ill-treatment at every turn, shootings, gallows-hanging and cruel punishment in public. Violence without limit reigned in the quarry close to the camp; the group of prisoners working in this place suffered the highest number of victims. They had to quarry the material used for the foundation in roadmaking while others carried it to its destination with nothing but the help of their bare hands. Any show of open resistance to ill-treatment and humiliation ended in the cells of the "Bunker".

During the first years, the SS were mainly concerned with their housing, training and service facilities being built. Comfortable houses for the SS commanders, a falcon house and even a zoo were built in addition to the barracks.

The First Years of the War

Buchenwald Concentration Camp saw the biggest increase among all concentration camps existing in the German Reich with the arrival of 8463 persons during the weeks of September and October 1939. Transports came from Poland, from occupied Austria, from the Gestapo offices in central Germany and from the concentration camp of Dachau near Munich. This mass arrival led to the eruption of the largest dysentery epidemic up to this time. It broke out in a tent camp adjoining the mustering ground. The SS isolated this provisional camp which was overcrowded with Austrian Jews and Poles and allowed the majority of the inmates to die from hunger and cold. The first crematorium in the camp was built in the context of this mass killing.

The wave of new prisoners arriving in 1939 was followed by transports from Poland in 1940 and 1941. Some of them came by way of Dachau concentration camp. Transports of Dutch hostages arrived in the second half of 1940 and a transport of Dutch Jews at the beginning of 1941. The construction of the prisoners' camp and of the SS facilities was essentially completed by 1941 and 1942. The Deutsche Ausrüstungswerke GmbH (DAW), a company owned by the SS acquired the camp workshops situated to the east of the camp fence in September 1940. It employed almost 500 prisoners by the end of 1940.

The genocide of Jews, Sinti and Romany Gypsies started in the extermination camps established on occupied Polish territory after the attack on the Soviet Union. The SS transported almost 600 prisoners from Buchenwald to the killing establishments in Sonnenstein and Bernburg in July 1941 and in March 1942. Most of them were Jews and they were suffocated to death in gas chambers. Most of the Jews who were spared from this murderous action were deported to Auschwitz extermination camp a couple of months later. The systematic mass murder of Soviet prisoners of war and the killing of patients suffering from tuberculosis started by using injections in Buchenwald itself.

Manpower for Armament

Every year of the war took more Austrians, Czechs, Poles, Dutchmen, Frenchmen, Belgians, Russians, Ukrainians, Jews, Sinti and Romany Gypsies, and finally people from almost every European country to the concentration camp of Buchenwald. The prisoners' community was joined by partisans, resistance fighters and prisoners of war from various nations. Other people were simply rounded up arbitrarily and deported to this place from towns and regions all over Europe. Germans had been a minority in the camp since 1942. The number of prisoners in Buchenwald concentration camp and in its external sites increased from 11,275 at the end of January 1943 to 37,319 at the end of the year and to 84,505 at the end of September 1944. The concentration camps turned into a giant reservoir of forced labour where huge masses of people were shifted from place to place. The SS leased prisoners to big German companies acting as representatives of the German Reich.

Extensions were built to the prisoners' camp and to the industrial facilities of Buchenwald. An armament factory and a railway station were created along the access road. Training units of the *Waffen-SS* moved into the new troop barracks built near the quarry. Provisional accommodations called the Small Camp were established on the northern side of the prisoners' camp. Buchenwald covered a built-up area of 190 hectares in the summer of 1944. This was its greatest extent. A network of external sites stretched across the area between the Elbe and the Rhine. Each of them constituted a concentration camp functioning in its own right.

The interest of the SS in having an efficient administration capable of running the huge camp and its external sites and the long perseverance of the political prisoners enabled German political prisoners to take over the most important functions available to prisoners in 1942 and 1943. This also created room for manoeuver for the international resistance organizations. Their centre was the International Camp Committee led by communists. Prisoners of diverse backgrounds made an effort to prevent the law of the jungle from being the only law in operation under these inhuman conditions. The rescue of more than 900 children and young people is one of the achievements of the resistance organization. Various national groups of prisoners set up committees of mutual aid and solidarity to help in the daily fight for survival, including e.g. the Comité des intérêts français and the Italian Solidarity. Hence, even a conversation, a shared piece of bread, a gesture of solidarity or a word of encouragement could be essential to keep up the strength of the individual.

The Last Months

The allied air-raid on the armament factory and the SS barracks destroyed many buildings outside the camp on 24th August 1944 and signalled the last period in the history of Buchenwald Concentration Camp. Trains carrying Hungarian and Polish Jews from Auschwitz, and French, Dutch, Norwegian, Danish and Belgian prisoners arrived almost every day in the weeks before and after the attack. Forced labour debilitated them of their physical and spiritual energies, extinguishing their lives. In September 1944, Buchenwald Concentration Camp took over the administration of the external camps belonging to the concentration camp for women in Ravensbrück. These sites were situated in Saxony, Thuringia, Hesse and in the Rhine country. They comprised more than 20,000 women. A big external site called "Dora" was part of the rocket production facilities located in underground galleries in the Harz mountains. It comprised more than 30,000 prisoners and assumed the status of an independent concentration camp in October 1944. But the number of prisoners in Buchenwald continued to rise in spite of this. It was the biggest among the concentration camps still in existence numbering 110,000 prisoners (85,000 men and 25,000 women) at the end of January 1945.

At this time, the big camps in the East were already in a state of dissolution. Tens of thousands of completely exhausted people, mostly Jews, arrived at the railway station of Buchenwald coming from the concentration camps of Auschwitz and Gross Rosen, from ghettos and forced labour camps. These carriages were full of dead people whose names have remained unknown. Those still alive were stuffed into the Small Camp under conditions that deteriorated daily. More than 13,000 people died in Buchenwald within a period of just 100 days at the beginning of 1945.

About 48,000 people, the highest number up to this time, stayed in the camp barracks in an area of just 40 hectares on Ettersberg Hill as the Allied front approached the camp at the beginning of April. The SS forced more than half of them to leave on evacuation marches at the last minute; the last journey for many of them.

In these April days, the camp resistance organization tried to delay the departure of these convoys. They managed to hide hundreds of people, including many Jews. But the resistance groups formed by the prisoners did not wait for the arrival of the liberators in a passive way. They rather used the first moments of their presence in the area still being fought over in order to occupy the watchtowers, hoist the white flag and safeguard the camp for two days. More than 21,000 people were in the camp when the first tanks of the 3rd US Army arrived in the camp on 11th of April.

COLIN DAVIS ON WIESEL'S NARRATIVE TECHNIQUES

La Nuit [*Night*] does not offer unmediated, uninterpreted realities. Events are filtered through the eyes of a narrator, Eliezer, whose primary function is to seize their meaning as he organizes them into a coherent narrative. He exhibits considerable control in his organization of material. The nine short chapters divide the text into manageable units that can be summarized as follows:

Chapter 1. In Sighet. Buildup to deportation.
Chapter 2. In train. Arrival in Birkenau.
Chapter 3. First experiences of Auschwitz. Transfer to Buna.
Chapter 4. Life in Buna. Hangings.
Chapter 5. Selections. Evacuation of camp.
Chapter 6. Evacuation through snow. Arrival in Gleiwitz.
Chapter 7. In train to Buchenwald.
Chapter 8. Death of father.
Chapter 9. Liberation of Buchenwald.

Throughout *La Nuit* Wiesel uses the past historic tense as part of a retrospective narrative. He is "telling a story" in a way that becomes more problematic in his later, more formally sophisticated fiction, with its changing narrative voices, shifting time scales, and unstable tense systems. In *La Nuit* the past historic gives the narrator retrospective command over his material. This allows him to organize and underline its significance, as well as to calculate and control its effect on the reader. Since this narrative mastery is important to the central tension of *La Nuit*, it is worth briefly describing some of the means by which it is achieved.

Direct comment. The narrator interrupts his description of events and comments directly; for example, while life for the

Jews in the ghetto is still relatively tolerable, the narrator shows the wisdom of hindsight:

> It was neither the German nor the Jew who reigned over the ghetto: it was illusion.

Reader's knowledge of history. Much of *La Nuit* is written in a terse, telegraphic style. Eliezer avoids commentary or explanation when the reader's knowledge of history can be expected to fill in gaps. The use of place names provides a clear example:

> But we arrived at a station. Those who were near the windows told us the name of the station:
> —Auschwitz.
> No one had ever heard that name.

> In front of us, those flames. In the air, that smell of burnt flesh. It must have been midnight. We had arrived. At Birkenau.

Warning and premonition. The Jews of Sighet are constantly being warned of what will happen to them. Moché recounts the atrocities of the Nazis, but is not believed. In the train to Auschwitz Mme Schächter has a premonitory vision ("—A fire! I can see a fire! I can see a fire!"), but she is bound, gagged, and beaten up by the other Jews. Later, the Jews are told what will happen to them:

> Sons of dogs, do you understand nothing then? You're going to be burned! Burned to a cinder! Turned to ashes!

Eliezer's direct comments also have a premonitory function:

> From that moment everything happened with great speed. The chase toward death had begun.

Retrospective viewpoint. Related to the latter point is the way in which the narrator can explain what he did not know at the time of the events being described due to knowledge acquired in the period between experiencing and describing. He uses phrases like "Later we were to learn," "I learned later," "I learned after the war," "Many years later."

Repetition of themes. One of the central concerns of *La Nuit* is Eliezer's relationship with his father and his ambiguous sense of guilt and liberation when his father dies. Eliezer's feeling that he has betrayed his father is reflected in other father-son relationships that he compulsively describes. Béla Katz, seconded to the *Sonder-Kommando*, places his own father's body into the furnace at Birkenau; the narrator refers to a child who beats his father; during the long march from Buna to Gleiwitz, Rabbi Eliahou is left behind by his son, who has run on ahead, Eliezer believes, "in order to free himself from that burden that could reduce his own chances of survival"; and on the train to Buchenwald, a man murders his own father for the sake of a piece of bread.

Preparation of effects. Eliezer introduces striking or unexpected details that seem out of place at first, but that reinforce the impact of what comes later. After the first execution that he witnesses, Eliezer seems unmoved: "I remember that that evening I found the soup excellent . . ."; later, the cruel execution of a young boy is interpreted as reflecting the death of God, and Eliezer picks up his words from the previous page: "That evening, the soup had the taste of a corpse." In Buna the treatment of the children seems to indicate a more humane attitude than we had been led to expect:

> Our convoy contained several children of ten, twelve years of age. The officer took an interest in them and ordered that some food be brought for them.

A page later, a more sinister explanation for the officer's interest is suggested as a new character is introduced:

> Our block leader was a German [. . .] Like the head of
> the camp, he liked children. Immediately after our arrival
> he had had some bread, soup and margarine brought
> for them (in reality, this affection was not disinterested:
> children here were the object, amongst homosexuals, of a
> real trade, as I was to learn later).

Through these devices, the narrator filters, interprets, and
assimilates the experience of the Holocaust. Wiesel adopts
a form and techniques that seem to confirm the Jewish
expectation of the meaning of history and the interpretability
of experience. The essential problem of *La Nuit* derives from
the tension between the formal coherence and retrospective
authority of the narrative, and the subject-matter of the work.
Wiesel has always emphasized that the Holocaust can be
neither understood nor described; it is a unique event without
precedent, parallel, analogy, or meaning. This results in a
problem of communication, and the survivors' predicament
is particularly acute. They must, and cannot, recount the
experience of the death camps: "Impossible to speak of it,
impossible not to speak of it." *La Nuit*, then, is written in the
knowledge of its own inevitable failure: the survivor must
tell his story, but will never communicate the truth of his
experience; what is kept silent is more true than what is said,
words distort and betray, the Holocaust cannot be understood
or described. . . .

The fundamental double bind at the core of Wiesel's
writing lies in the fact that he must and cannot write about the
Holocaust. His experiences during the war are at the source of
his urge to narrate and to bear witness; at the same time, those
experiences corrode the foundation of his narrative art as they
undermine faith in mankind, God, self, and language. *La Nuit*
is a work sustained by its own impossibility: the need to tell
the truth about something that entails a crisis of belief in truth.
The tension of *La Nuit* lies in its simultaneous assertion that
what it narrates is true and that it cannot be true; such events
cannot be perpetrated or seen or described. The narrator wants
to believe he is mistaken at the very moment when he claims

to be most brutally honest. So *La Nuit*, despite its apparent simplicity, is a deeply paradoxical work; a first-person narrative that recounts the destruction of identity, . . . a coherent account of the collapse of coherence, an attempt to describe what the author of the text insists cannot be described.

SIMON P. SIBELMAN ON THE ROLE OF TIME IN THE BOOK

The first element of life that must be silenced is time. Time lies at the heart of existence, a principle particularly true in Jewish thought and teachings. Abraham Joshua Heschel notes that "Judaism is a religion of time aiming at the sanctification of time." So it is that at the beginning of *La Nuit* [*Night*], time meticulously and meaningfully guides the young protagonist through life, through his studies and prayers. Time is represented as a creative force, a bridge linking man to eternity.

The first incursion of night into the harmonious passage of time is the deportation and subsequent return of Moché-le-Bedeau. The destructive silence of the Jewish tragedy has taken its toll. . . . "He closed his eyes, as though to escape time." More importantly, this silencing of time brings with it other startling transformations. . . . "Moché had changed. There was no longer any joy in his eyes. He no longer sang. He no longer talked to me of God or the cabbala." As time is silenced, creativity ceases, and negative silence descends over life.

Moché's return not only marks the initial transformation of time, but it evokes a curious response from the Jewish community of Sighet. Moché (whose name is Moses), the prophet who has seen the advancing night, is viewed as being a madman. The Jews would prefer to purchase his silence, to erase his message. Ironically, Moché's purchased mutism only permits the Jews of Sighet to resume life behind a protective façade of silence that descends. But this brief contact with the night has unquestionably altered life. Though the Allied broadcasts offer a degree of hope, Wiesel underlies the text with a bitter irony: The utter silence of the Allies concerning the fate of Europe's Jewish population.

Though metamorphosing, time persists in its existence. With its natural passage the Nazis arrive. The course which would lead to Birkenau has been set in motion. Ghettos were established where life sought to maintain a degree of normalcy. Stories, part of the fabric of Jewish life, continued to be told. But . . . the good stories being told are silence and will remain forever unfinished. Words have lost their positive creative powers. The only remaining significant communication becomes nonverbal. Whereas time has previously stimulated creativity, it now stifles the word/Word. Time comes to represent a negative force, and even the "ongoing tale" is tainted by it. . . .

The final rupture of time occurs with the arrival of the deported Jews at Birkenau-Auschwitz. After a seemingly endless night in the stinking confines of the cattle cars, time ceases to exist as they enter the kingdom of night where all the imagined horrors of two millennia of Christian iconography become real. . . .

In *La Nuit*, time ceases to have a creative dimension and enters the realm of pure negativism. As Wiesel's work evolves, time will remain fragmented as he passes from the world of the living to the domain of the dead. This particular feature produces a unique literary structure that will facilitate the blending of the past, present, and future, and will reinforce the notion of the instantaneous multiplicity of various levels of perception and significance.

Wiesel's use of time and fragmented structure firmly entrench his oeuvre within the traditions of contemporary writers, . . . The role of the writer has been radically altered. Beliefs in former literary dogmas, which has propounded a faith in the unshakable nature of civilization, can no longer be supported. As a result, chronological time as a traditional aspect of storytelling can no longer be viewed as an ally; it has become a menacing shadow. Time has been equaled to man's perception of reality. Moreover, after Auschwitz, reality could no longer be viewed as before. For Jean Cayrol, this fact represents perhaps the most influential element in the creation of modern literature. He discerns aspects of the [world of the concentration camp] within all men. The fragmentation of linear time permits the past inexorably to become part of the future. Thus one can view Wiesel's use of this technique as representing his adherence to current literary trends, as well as serving as a universal reminder of those events that produced the initial rupture. Moreover, one must also view Wiesel's perception of time as being reflective of his own Hasidic background. Hasidic stories do not adhere to occidental conventions of temporal exigencies, but create notions of time that are subordinated to the message of the tale. Metaphysics and mystery reign, and the storyteller manipulates past and present to enhance particular moral themes.

As time is closely related to our understanding of reality, its silencing must therefore effect the existence and perception of truth. As previously noted, when Moché-le-Bedeau returned from his deportation and sought to warn the Jews of Sighet . . . no one would believe him. His vision of truth could not be accommodated within a traditional temporal framework. This attitude is strengthened when, during the journey to Auschwitz, Moché's words are echoed and even intensified in the frightening prophetic ravings of Mme. Schächter. . . . Nevertheless Mme. Schächter's prophesies, like those of Jeremiah, become an unbearable reality as the sealed train arrives at Birkenau.

Eliezer has come to exist within a timeless void from which truth has been exiled or deformed. In this silent wasteland, he will suffer the destruction of his own beliefs in a just and true God, as well as in the goodness of fellow human beings.

ORA AVNI ON NARRATIVE AND THE BURDEN OF WITNESS

Night is the story of a young boy's journey through hell, as he is taken first to a ghetto, and then to Auschwitz and Buchenwald. It is a story of survival and of death: survival of the young narrator himself, but death of the world as he knew it. It is therefore a negative *Bildungsroman*, in which the character does not end up, as expected, fit for life in society, but on the contrary, a living dead, unfit for life as defined by his community.

Its opening focuses not so much on the boy, however, as on a foreigner, Moshe the Beadle, a wretched yet good-natured and lovable dreamer, versed in Jewish mysticism. When the town's foreign Jews are deported by the Nazis to an unknown destination, he leaves with them; but he comes back. Having miraculously survived the murder of his convoy, he hurries back to warn the others. No longer singing, humming, or praying, he plods from door to door, desperately repeating the same stories of calm and dispassionate killings. But, despite his unrelenting efforts, "people refused not only to believe his stories, but even to listen to them."

Like Moshe the Beadle, the first survivors who told their stories either to other Jews or to the world were usually met with disbelief. When the first escapees from Ponar's killing grounds tried to warn the Vilna ghetto that they were not sent to work but to be murdered, not only did Jews not believe them, but they accused the survivors of demoralizing the ghetto, and demanded that they stop spreading such stories. Similarly, when Jan Karski, the courier of the Polish government-in-exile who had smuggled himself into the Warsaw Ghetto so that he could report the Nazis' atrocities as an eyewitness, made his report to Justice Felix Frankfurter, the latter simply said, "I don't believe you." Asked to explain, he added, "I did not say that this young man is lying. I said I cannot believe him. There is a difference." How are we to understand this disbelief? What are its causes and effects, and above all, what lesson can we learn from it. . . .

The Subject in History
Our critique of the psychoanalytic approach relies on our view of the object's self-positioning in history, at once in the privacy of his inner world, in the limited exchange set with one's interlocutor (say, a therapist), and mostly, in the larger context of stories we tell ourselves versus stories into which we are born. The exemplary value of *Night*'s opening episode hinges upon its containing the narrative of the boy, and by

extension of any survivor, within the problems raised by this self-positioning.

Prior to his own encounter with Nazism, the boy asks Moshe: "Why are you so anxious that people should believe what you say? In your place, I shouldn't care whether they believe me or not. . . ." Indeed, in comparison with the ordeal from which he has just escaped, there seems to be little reason for Moshe's present distress. What, then, hangs upon the credibility of his story? Why do the town people refuse to listen to the beadle? What effect does their reaction have on the *project* that brought him back to town? . . .

Moshe's anguished insistence on being heard undoubtedly illustrates the well-known recourse to narrative in order to impose coherence on an incoherent experience (a commonplace of literary criticism), to work through a trauma (a commonplace of psychoanalysis), the laudable drive to testify to a crime (a commonplace of *Shoah* narratives), or even the heroics of saving others (a commonplace of resistance literature). Although such readings of *Night* are certainly not irrelevant, I do not think that they do justice to the gripping urgency of his unwelcome and redundant narrative, unless we read the text literally: Moshe came back "to tell you the story."

We must rule out simply imparting knowledge, since Moshe's undertaking clearly does not stop at communicating the story. A scenario in which the town folks gather around him to listen to his story, and then go on about their business would be absurd. In this case, to "believe" the story is to be affected by it. Moshe's story is therefore a speech act. . . .

Speech act theorists unanimously agree on the conventional aspect of a speech act, that is, on its reliance on a preexisting convention shared by the community of its listeners. But sometimes, such a precise convention does not exist. It has to be inferred and activated out of the stock of beliefs and conventions that both utterer and listeners find workable, plausible, and altogether acceptable. In invoking their shared beliefs, the felicitous speech act thus becomes a *rallying point* for the utterer and the listeners. Iit binds them together. A community is therefore as much the *result* of its speech acts as it is the necessary condition for their success. In other words, if, as he claims, Moshe came back to town in order to tell his story, and if indeed he is determined to secure the felicitous uptake of his narrative's illocutionary force, then this determination reveals yet *another project*, one that is even more exacting in that it affects his (and his fellow villagers') being-in-the-world: his return to town is also an attempt to reaffirm his ties to his community (its conventions, its values), to reintegrate into the human community of his past—a community whose integrity was put into question by the absurd, incomprehensible, and unassimilable killings he has witnessed. Through his encounter with Nazism, Moshe has witnessed not only the slaughter of human cargo, but the demise of his notion of humanity—a notion, however, still shared by the town folks. As long as they hold on to this notion of humanity to which he can no longer adhere, he is, *ipso facto*, a freak. Coming back to town to tell his story to a receptive audience is therefore Moshe's way back to normalcy, back to humanity. Only by having a community integrate his dehumanizing experience into the narratives of self-representation that it shares and infer a new code of behavior based on the information he is imparting, only by becoming part of his community's history, can Moshe hope to reclaim his lost humanity (the question remains, as we shall see, at what price to his community). It is therefore not a question of privately telling the story (to oneself, to one's editor or to one's analyst) as of having others—a whole community—*claim* it, *appropriate* it, and *react* (properly) to it.

The closing scene of *Night* echoes this concern. Upon his liberation by American troops, the narrator first rushes to a mirror to look at himself. Is he still himself? Can the mirror show him unchanged since the last time he looked at himself in the mirror, before he was taken out of his village? Can he reintegrate into himself? Will the mirror allow him to bridge over pain and time, and reach the cathartic recognition that will bracket out the horror of the death camps and open the way for a "normal" life; or will it, on the contrary, irreparably clinch his alienation not only from the world but from the supposed intimacy of his self-knowledge? Like Moshe then, the boy leaves it to a third party (a willing community or a mirror) to mediate between his present and past selves, and cancel out the alienating effect of his brush with inhumanity. Just like the town folks, however, the mirror does not cooperate. Instead of the familiar face that would have reconciled him with his former self, . . . his reflection seals his alienation: "From the depth of the mirror, a corpse gazed back at me. The look in his eyes, as they stared into mine, has never left me."

Night is the story of a repeated dying, at once the death of man and of the *idea* of man. The final recognition never obtains. Instead, the subject is propelled out of himself, out of humanity, out of the world as he knew it. It is a double failure: both Moshe and the boy fail to recover their selves' integrity and to reintegrate into the community of the living; both fail to assimilate the traces left by their experience . . . into a coherent picture to be accepted by the other(s) they so wish to reach. But the story goes on: *Night* is a first-person narrative. Like Moshe, the boy will try again to reintegrate the human community, this time, by telling his story (and many others). Like all survivors' narratives, *Night* is thus yet another plodding from door to door to solicit listeners, so as to reclaim one's ties to the community of the living by inscribing oneself into its shared narratives.

RUTH FRANKLIN RE-EVALUATES *NIGHT*

Night is the most devastating account of the Holocaust that I have ever read. It is devastating first because of its simplicity. The basic outline is this: after the Germans invade Hungary in 1944, the teenaged Eliezer and his family, religious Jews who live comfortably in their community, are deported to Auschwitz. He and his father, separated from the rest of their family, are assigned to hard labor. As the last days of the war endlessly tick by, they survive transfers, work assignments, selections, illnesses, and all the other daily threats of life in the camp, while watching their friends and neighbors fall dead all around them. In January 1945, Auschwitz is liquidated, and they march through the snow for days before being transferred to Buchenwald. There Eliezer watches his father slowly die.

There are no epiphanies in *Night*, like Primo Levi's epiphany in *Survival in Auschwitz*, when he recalls the story of Ulysses from Dante's *Inferno* and remembers that he, too, is a thinking, feeling human being. And there is no irony, like Imre Kertész's irony in *Fatelessness*, when the narrator, mistaken for a corpse and carted away, protests that he would "like to live a bit longer in this beautiful concentration camp." There is no extraneous detail, no analysis, no speculation. There is only a story: Eliezer's account of what happened, spoken in his voice.

The story itself is by now familiar. We know all about Dr. Mengele and people being sent to the left and to the right, about the Zyklon B and the crematoria, about the bizarre systems and hierarchies that allowed some prisoners to discover methods of survival and condemned others to an even quicker death. And the story's familiarity etherizes our minds into complacency: it becomes possible for us to think that because we know about all these things, we actually *know* them. Auschwitz is no longer just a place—it is a shorthand for the Shoah, a common metaphor for uncommon evil, the almost platitudinous reference for the very embodiment of hell on earth.

Amazingly, such complacency had already set in just a decade after the war, when François Mauriac wrote in his foreword to the French edition of *Night* that "this personal record, coming after so many others and describing an outrage about which we might imagine we already know all that it is possible to know, is nevertheless different, distinct, unique." He suggested that *Night*'s uniqueness resides in the circumstances of its coming to exist—that is, its author's experiences during the war years—which "would in themselves be sufficient to inspire a book to which no other could be compared."

By this standard, however, every Holocaust memoir is "unique," since each survivor tells his or her own terrible story. The second reason *Night* is incomparably devastating has less to do with the facts of Wiesel's story than with the way he tells them. The book is exquisitely constructed. I do not mean that it is beautifully written: its language and style are decidedly plain. But every sentence feels weighted and deliberate, every episode carefully chosen and delineated. It is also shockingly brief; it can be read in an hour, and carried in a pocket. One has the sense of merciless experience mercilessly distilled to its essence, because to take a story as fundamentally brutal as this one and clutter it with embellishments would be grotesque. By refusing to add the rationality of explanation or the cynicism of hindsight, *Night* takes us back to its terrible story with something resembling innocence, the innocence of a young boy who, like the rest of the Jews of Europe, had no idea what was coming. To read it is to lose one's own innocence about the Holocaust all over again.

Night, together with *The Diary of Anne Frank*, told the story of the Holocaust to the world. The book has been translated into thirty languages and has sold more than six million copies in the United States alone. When the American edition appeared, A. Alvarez wrote in *Commentary* that it was "almost unbearably painful, and certainly beyond criticism." In the years since then, *Night*'s potency has been diffused by its very canonicity. It has been relegated to high school reading lists and overshadowed by the subsequent fame of its author. But now a new chapter has opened in *Night*'s strange career. A lucid new translation of the book by Marion Wiesel, the author's wife, has been selected by Oprah Winfrey for her influential book club; and last month, nearly a half-century after its publication, *Night* made its first appearance at the top of the *New York Times* best-seller list.

Night's resuscitation comes at a difficult time for the genre of memoir, which has lately been undergoing a crisis. First James Frey was embraced and then flagellated by Winfrey for fabricating large parts of *A Million Little Pieces*; and soon several other opportunists who had fraudulently claimed an autobiographical basis for their fiction were similarly debunked. Considering the circumstances, Winfrey's endorsement of *Night* was a canny move: what could better restore her credibility—and the credibility of memoir itself—than a book that was "beyond criticism"? And in fact *Night* was seized as a lodestar of authenticity by the many commentators who lambasted Winfrey's judgment in the Frey affair. Frank Rich even suggested, quite preposterously, that Winfrey's initial support of the dissimulator Frey might be used by Holocaust deniers to discount Wiesel's experiences.

Unfortunately, *Night* is an imperfect ambassador for the infallibility of the memoir, for the simple fact that it has itself often been treated as a novel—by journalists, by scholars, and even by its publishers. Matters are further confused by Wiesel's admission in the preface to the new edition that, thanks to his wife's editing, he had been able "to correct and revise a number of important details." He does not elaborate on what these details are, but the statement was quickly investigated by the news media, which reported that among them are such errors as the narrator's age upon his arrival at Auschwitz. (In the first English translation he is said to be "almost fifteen," while in the new edition he is fifteen.) Understandably embarrassed by any suggestion of similarity between his book and Frey's, Wiesel asserted to a reporter that since *Night* is a memoir, his "experiences in the book—A to Z—must be true. . . . I object angrily if someone mentions it as a novel."

But if *Night* is not a novel, even an autobiographical novel, it is not exactly a memoir, either—if one defines memoir, following Michiko Kakutani (one of the many to go mildly nuts about Frey's hoax) as a form that prizes "authenticity above all else." In our present circumstances, the book has a useful lesson to teach about the complexities of memoir and memory. The story of how *Night* came into existence reveals just how many factors come into play in the creation of a memoir—the obligation to remember and to testify, certainly, but also the artistic and even moral obligation to construct a credible persona and to craft a beautiful work. Fact, we know, can be stranger than fiction; but truth in prose, it turns out, is not always the same thing as truth in life.

Night was first published in Buenos Aires in 1956, as the 117th volume in a series of Yiddish memoirs of prewar and wartime Europe, under the title ". . . un di velt hot geshvign," or . . . *And the World Was Silent*. Ruth R. Wisse, in *The Modern Jewish Canon*, notes that in contrast to the other works in the series, which were traditional testimonials that aimed to memorialize as many of the murdered as possible, Wiesel's book was a "highly selective and isolating literary narrative" clearly influenced by its young author's reading of the French existentialists. When the book was translated (or as Wisse puts it, "transposed") into French, this distinction sharpened, beginning with the title, which shifts the book's emphasis from the silence of the world at the Jews' fate to the abstract "night," which can mean at once the darkness of the camps and the moral and spiritual darkness of the world during (and after) World War II. Wiesel was re-imagining his book not for his shrinking Yiddish readership, but for the global audience that it would eventually attain.

Wiesel's Yiddish manuscript was more than eight hundred pages long. *La Nuit*, as it was published by Éditions du Minuit in 1958, was 121 pages. Wiesel says that he made a number of the cuts on his own, with further editing from his French publisher, which he then approved. All material not directly related to the story was pruned away. "Substance alone mattered," Wiesel writes in the preface to the new edition (which, like all the translations of *Night*, is based on the French version, not the Yiddish original). "I was more afraid of having said too much than too little." But his revisions had other implications as well. As Naomi Seidman wrote in an essay called "Elie Wiesel and the Scandal of Jewish Rage," which analyzes some of Wiesel's revisions to the Yiddish text, "There are two survivors . . . a Yiddish and a French": the first wrote a testimonial that was largely intended for the historical record, while the second had grander ambitions.

The book originally began with a passage in which the author, in lines steeped in his biblical education, lamented the Jews' self-deception during the war years:

In the beginning there was faith—which is childish; trust—which is vain; and illusion—which is dangerous.

We believed in God, trusted in man, and lived with the illusion that every one of us has been entrusted with a sacred spark from the Shekhinah's flame; that every one of us carries in his eyes and in his soul a reflection of God's image.

That was the source if not the cause of all our ordeals.

And it ended with what Wiesel calls a "gloomy meditation" on the global response to the Holocaust:

Now, scarcely ten years after Buchenwald, I realize that the world forgets quickly. Today, Germany is a sovereign state. The German army has been resuscitated. Ilse Koch, the notorious sadistic monster of Buchenwald, was allowed to have children and live happily ever after . . . War criminals stroll through the streets of Hamburg and Munich. The past seems to have been erased, relegated to oblivion.

Today, there are anti-Semites in Germany, France, and even the United States who tell the world that the "story" of six million assassinated Jews is nothing but a hoax, and many people, not knowing any better, may well believe them, if not today then tomorrow or the day after. . . .

As Wisse points out, there is a political purpose to the disappearance of these lines from the text: Wiesel may have been reluctant to expose the "collective self-blame" of the Jews or his own fury at the rest of the world to a primarily Gentile audience. But, more importantly, there is an aesthetic imperative at work as well. These passages have their own didactic power: Wiesel's bitterness as he speaks of the Jews' belief as an "illusion," and his expression of his own impotence in the face of Holocaust denial, is tragic. But their moralizing tone is at odds with the simplicity of the main narrative, and it detracts from the power of the story. There is a terrifying finality to the last scene of the edited version, in which the narrator, after the liberation of Buchenwald and a brief stay in the hospital, looks at himself in the mirror for the first time since his imprisonment: "From the depths of the mirror, a corpse was contemplating me. The look in his eyes as he gazed at me has never left me." This otherworldly image is worth a thousand words about the lack of justice for the Nazis or the continuing anti-Semitism of Holocaust deniers.

Like any memoir, *Night* must balance between absolute fidelity to the events and the making of literature. Its poetic austerity comes at a cost to the literal truth. This cost, it must be said, does not detract in the least way from *Night's* validity as a Holocaust testimonial. (Since Seidman published her essay about Wiesel ten years ago, it has been outrageously appropriated by Holocaust deniers who exploit her analysis of the differences between Wiesel's Yiddish and French texts for their own purposes.) But it is worth recognizing that such a cost exists, if only to remind ourselves that no memoir can be at once an unerring representation of reality and a genuine artistic achievement.

Consider, for example, the book's first chapter, which begins in 1942, when Eliezer (as the narrator of *Night* calls himself) is twelve years old. He describes himself as "deeply observant" and immersed in religious study, though he has been unable to find anyone willing to tutor him in kabbalah, an esoteric subject of study generally restricted to older men. One day at the synagogue he falls into conversation with Moishe the Beadle, a poor man who reveals a surprising fount of knowledge. Eliezer recounts one of their dialogues:

> Man comes closer to God through the questions he asks Him, he liked to say. Therein lies true dialogue. Man asks and God replies. But we don't understand His replies. We cannot understand them. Because they dwell in the depths of our souls and remain there until we die. The real answers, Eliezer, you will find only within yourself.
> "And why do you pray, Moishe?" I asked him.
> "I pray to the God within me for the strength to ask Him the real questions." . . .
> And in the course of those evenings I became convinced that Moishe the Beadle would help me enter eternity, into that time when question and answer would become ONE.

These talks end when Moishe, along with the rest of the town's foreign Jews, is deported.

He returns with a horrifying tale. The Jews, he said, traveled first by train and then by truck to a forest in Galicia, where they were forced to dig trenches. After they had finished, they were shot one by one. Moishe escaped, miraculously, after being wounded in the leg and left for dead. But no matter how many times he repeats his story, no one believes him; even as late as the spring of 1944, as German troops are invading Budapest, the Jews of Sighet do not think the army will reach their town. They do not even really believe that Hitler intends to exterminate the Jews. The narrator does not try to explain their naïveté, just as later he does not try to explain the Nazis' brutality. He relies only on factual statements: "In less than three days, German army vehicles made their appearance on our streets."

"Night fell. . . . Night had fallen. . . . Night." This is the book's only narrative flourish: an almost incantatory repetition, in steady but irregular beats at the beginning of a sentence or a passage bearing some new agony. The Jews of Sighet are first restricted to two small ghettos; soon they learn they are all to be deported. Eliezer's family is in the last group to go, packed eighty to a train car. In their car is a woman named Mrs. Schächter, who has lost her mind and cries out continually: "Fire! I see a fire! I see flames, huge flames!" The other passengers tie her down and gag her. Finally they arrive at a train station bearing the sign "Auschwitz." Here Mrs. Schächter screams of fire again, and now the rest of the passengers see it too.

Is it not too much to ask that the impoverished beadle be both a master of the kabbalah and a Cassandra-like figure whose warnings go unheeded? Or, similarly, that the journey to Auschwitz be punctuated by the cries of another unacknowledged clairvoyant? In fact, if one compares the events in *Night* to Wiesel's account of his wartime experience in his memoirs, the first part of which were published in 1996 under the title *All Rivers Run to the Sea*, the evidence of artistic labor can easily be found. The young Wiesel, who was brought up in the hasidic tradition, did in fact dabble in Jewish mysticism, but his master was a man named Kalman, not Moishe the beadle, who is another person entirely. The character in *Night* is a composite, and so the dialogue that Wiesel reports, and which I quoted above, must be imagined. Mrs. Schächter and her terrifying vision appears in both books, but in *All Rivers Run to the Sea* she merits just a single mention, while her role in *Night* is considerably upgraded. Then there is all the information that appears in the memoirs but did not find its way into *Night*, including the warnings that the Jews of Sighet did have and the repeated deliberations they made about what to do.

Does anybody, other than the literary scholar, care about such variations? Do they matter in any way? They are not problems of fact, after all; they are instances of artistic license. And that is precisely why they are important. Wiesel's decision to make the beadle a secret kabbalist sacrifices literal fact for literary effect: it simplifies the story, helping it to achieve its parable-like quality, and it adds another dimension to Moishe's tragedy. It indicates that Wiesel recognizes the memoirist's dual obligation—to the truth, certainly, but also to tell his story in the most interesting, most memorable, and most meaningful way possible. Like the translator who occasionally veers from the grammar of an individual phrase for the sake of the quality of the whole work, the memoirist too must have the liberty to shape his raw materials into a work of art.

Wiesel's shaping occurs mainly in the service of the narrator's crisis of faith, which is the basso continuo beneath the entire book. It is embodied in *Night*'s central episode: the public hanging of a young boy with an angelic face, who served as one of the Kapos' assistants, together with two other men. Here is Ruth R. Wisse's translation of the scene as it appears in the original Yiddish manuscript:

> Both adults were already dead. The noose had choked them at once. Instantly they expired. Their extended tongues were red as fire.

The slight Jewish child with the lost dreamy eyes was still alive. His body weighed too little. Was too light. The noose didn't "catch."

The slow death of the little *meshoresl* [assistant] took thirty-five minutes. And we saw him wobbling, swaying, on the rope, with his bluish-red tongue extended, with a prayer on his grey-white lips, a prayer to God, to the Angel of Death, to take pity on him, to take his soul, liberating it from its death-throes, from the torments of the grave. When we saw him like that, the hanged child, many of us didn't want to, couldn't keep from crying.

—Where is God?—the same man asked again, behind me. Something in me wanted to answer him:

—Where is God? Here he is, hanging on the gallows ... [ellipsis in original]

That evening the soup had no taste.

We hid it away for the next day.

And here it is in *Night*, in Marion Wiesel's translation:

The two men were no longer alive. Their tongues were hanging out, swollen and bluish. But the third rope was still moving: the child, too light, was still breathing ... [ellipsis in original]

And so he remained for more than half an hour, lingering between life and death, writhing before our eyes. And we were forced to look at him at close range. He was still alive when I passed him. His tongue was still red, his eyes not yet extinguished.

Behind me, I heard the same man asking:

"For God's sake, where is God?"

And from within me, I heard a voice answer:

"Where He is? This is where—hanging here from this gallows. . . ."

That night the soup tasted of corpses.

The "improved" version is shorter, most obviously, but it also speaks from a subtly altered perspective. The voice in the first passage is communal: "When we saw him . . . many of us . . . couldn't keep from crying." The second emphasizes the singular experience of the narrator: "He was still alive when I passed him." The Holocaust happened to a whole community, obviously, but the community cannot effectively speak as a whole. It is only with the voice of an individual messenger that we can empathize. The new version also boldly alters the final line. Wisse comments that the passage's new ending is "more credible," since "by all accounts, no one at Auschwitz could have left his soup for the next day." But her reading overlooks the fact that Wiesel has taken a simple description ("the soup had no taste") and substituted a literary trope ("the soup tasted of corpses"). Even at Auschwitz, corpses were not actually used to prepare the soup. Paradoxically, a metaphor becomes more believable than an unembellished description.

It is worth noting, though, that the substance of the passage—which is not altered at all in the translation into French and English—is a highly stylized scene constructed to maximize every bit of its shock value. As many critics have remarked, the execution of the angelic young boy together with two anonymous men has Christ-like overtones, which are heightened by the inherent similarity between the gallows and the crucifix. But even discounting this framework, the narrator bluntly informs us of the death of God, in phrasing that is strikingly similar in the two versions. The passage functions as a turning point in *Night*, after which the narrator apparently ceases to believe. Up to now, he has occasionally invoked God's presence, if only as bitter commentary. "How I sympathized with Job!" he comments early on. "I did not deny God's existence, but I doubted his absolute justice." But soon after the hanging the inmates celebrate Rosh Hashanah, and Eliezer feels unable to take part in the services. "Blessed be God's name?" he asks.

Why, but why would I bless Him? Every fiber in me rebelled. Because He caused thousands of children to burn in His mass graves? Because He kept six crematoria working day and night, including Sabbath and the Holy

Days? Because in His great might, He had created Auschwitz, Birkenau, Buna, and so many other factories of death? How could I say to Him: Blessed be Thou, Almighty, Master of the Universe, who chose us among all nations to be tortured day and night, to watch as our fathers, our mothers, our brothers end up in the furnaces? . . . But now, I no longer pleaded for anything. I was no longer able to lament. On the contrary, I felt very strong. I was the accuser, God the accused. My eyes had opened and I was alone, terribly alone in a world without God, without man.

In his memoir, Wiesel writes with some annoyance that *Night* has often been read as a narrative about the loss of faith. On the contrary, he says, he remained a believer after the war (and writes with joy of resuming his Talmudic studies at a camp for displaced children in France), and he continues to practice Judaism to this day. Yet what he has written in *Night* is more than an indictment of God's absence, along the lines of Paul Celan's famous poem "Tenebrae," in which the Jews in the camps address God in a tone that is half menacing, half sympathetic: "Pray, Lord, / Pray to us, / We are near"; or of Zvi Kolitz's legendary story "Yosl Rakover Talks to God," which imagines an extended soliloquy directed by a Jew in the Warsaw Ghetto to a God who has "hidden his face from the world." Indeed, after this point God nearly disappears from *Night*, returning only at the very end for one last plea. Watching an elderly rabbi search for the son who has abandoned him in the desperate snowy march from Auschwitz, Eliezer prays to "that God in whom I no longer believed: My God, Lord of the Universe, give me strength never to do what Rabbi Eliahou's son has done." His prayer, if it is heard, is not answered.

There is something a little barbaric about performing this sort of dissection on such a book. To be sure, questions have been raised in the past about Wiesel's report even by those who are not Holocaust deniers, specifically his original suggestion that couples "copulated" in the cattle cars on the way to Auschwitz (this was always a gross mistranslation of the original Yiddish, and the new version has toned it down to "caressed each other") and his claim that he saw living babies tossed into flaming pits on his first night in the camp, which has been challenged in *The New York Times Book Review* and elsewhere. In the foreword to the new edition, he insists that the latter claim is true. (Given everything we know about the sadism of the SS, what is so obviously suspicious about it?) But the very act of trying to put *Night* under the fact-checker's lens smacks of indecency. One cannot seriously worry about whether babies were burned alive or dead at Auschwitz without losing something of one's own humanity. Is it not enough to know that they were burned at all?

Wiesel, I suspect, would agree. Another passage cut from the Yiddish version describes the death of his father, which is the great tragedy of *Night*. "Why not include those [lines] in the new translation?" Wiesel asks in the foreword. "Too personal, too private, perhaps; they need to remain between the lines. And yet . . ." And he goes on to give the passage in its entirety, but separate from the main text. The material that was cut adds nothing to the factual content of the scene: it describes his feelings, his fear of the SS guard who was beating his father and thus his reluctance to come to his father's aid, and his shame at his own fear. The final version leaves all that to the reader's imagination:

> In front of the block, the SS were giving orders. An officer passed between the bunks. My father was pleading:
> "My son, water . . . I'm burning up . . . My insides . . ."
> "Silence over there!" barked the officer.
> "Eliezer," continued my father, "water . . ."
> The officer came closer and shouted to him to be silent. But my father did not hear. He continued to call me. The officer wielded his club and dealt him a violent blow to the head.
> I didn't move. I was afraid, my body was afraid of another blow, this time to *my* head.
> My father groaned once more, I heard:
> "Eliezer . . ."

I could see that he was still breathing—in gasps. I didn't move.

[all ellipses in original]

Is one version truer than the other? No one could say—not even, I suspect, Wiesel himself, which is precisely why he includes them both. "I mean to recount not the story of my life, but my stories," he writes in *All Rivers Run to the Sea*. "Some see their work as a commentary on their life; for others it is the other way around. I count myself among the latter. Consider this account, then, as a kind of commentary." The purpose of a commentary is to explicate—but also to invite discussion, argument, more commentary. As the young kabbalist in the death camps knows, the union of question and answer will take place only in eternity.

Works by Elie Wiesel

A Mad Desire to Dance, 2009.

The Time of the Uprooted: A Novel, 2005.

Wise Men and Their Tales, 2003.

The Judges: A Novel, 2002.

After the Darkness: Reflections on the Holocaust, 2002.

Conversations with Elie Wiesel, 2001.

King Solomon and His Magic Ring, 1999.

And the Sea Is Never Full: Memoirs, 1999.

The Fifth Son, 1998.

All Rivers Run to the Sea: Memoirs, 1996.

Memoir in Two Voices, with François Mitterrand, 1996.

A Passover Haggadah, 1993.

The Forgotten, 1992.

Sages and Dreamers, 1991.

Evil and Exile, 1990.

From the Kingdom of Memory: Reminiscences, 1990.

A Journey of Faith, with John Cardinal O'Connor, 1990.

Twilight, 1989.

The Six Days of Destruction: Meditations Toward Hope, with Albert Friedlander, 1988.

Against Silence, 1985.

From the Kingdom of Silence, 1984.

The Golem, 1983.

Somewhere a Master, 1982.

The Testament: A Novel, 1981.

Five Biblical Portraits, 1981.

Images from the Bible, 1980.

The Trial of God (as it was held on February 25, 1649, in Shamgorod): A Play in Three Acts, 1979.

Four Hasidic Masters, 1978.

A Jew Today, 1978

Messengers of God, 1976.

Zalmen, or the Madness of God, 1974.

Ani Maamin, 1973.

The Oath, 1973.

Souls on Fire, 1972.

A Beggar in Jerusalem: A Novel, 1970.

One Generation After, 1970.

Legends of Our Time, 1968.

The Gates of the Forest, 1966.

The Jews of Silence, 1966.

The Town Beyond the Wall, 1964.

Day, also published as *The Accident*, 1962.

Dawn, 1961.

Night, 1960.

La Nuit, 1958.

Un di velt hot geshvign (And the World Remained Silent), 1956.

Annotated Bibliography

Aaron, Frieda W. *Bearing the Unbearable: Yiddish and Polish Poetry in the Ghettos and Concentration Camps.* Albany, NY: State University of New York Press, 1990.

Aaron, a survivor of the Warsaw ghetto and Majdanek concentration camp, examines Yiddish and Polish poetry written by inmates in concentration camps not after the experience but at the time of imprisonment.

Berenbaum, Michael. *The Vision of the Void: Theological Reflections on the Works of Elie Wiesel.* Middletown, Conn.: Wesleyan University Press, 1979.

Berenbaum's study of Wiesel's confrontation with an absent God was reissued as *Elie Wiesel: God, the Holocaust, and the Children of Israel* in 1994.

Brown, Robert McAfee. *Elie Wiesel, Messenger to All Humanity.* South Bend, Ind.: University of Notre Dame Press, 1989.

A Protestant theologian, Brown discusses Wiesel's writings as spiritual texts.

Cargas, Harry J. *Harry James Cargas in Conversation with Elie Wiesel.* New York: Paulist Press, 1976.

An interview with Wiesel about his life and work.

Cargas, Harry J., ed. *Responses to Elie Wiesel: Critical Essays by Major Jewish and Christian Scholars.* New York: Persea Books, 1978.

A collection of essays by scholars and literary critics regarding Wiesel's early work, with emphasis on the theological implications of his writings.

Fine, Ellen S. *Legacy of Night: The Literary Universe of Elie Wiesel.* Albany, NY: State University of New York Press, 1982.

Fine discusses *Night* as a literary work in itself and its position at the center of Wiesel's body of work.

Franciosi, Robert, ed. *Elie Wiesel: Conversations*. Jackson: University Press of Mississippi, 2002.

A collection of previously published interviews with Wiesel.

Greenberg, Irving, and Alvin H. Rosenfeld, eds. *Confronting the Holocaust: The Impact of Elie Wiesel*. Bloomington: Indiana University Press, 1978.

Anthology of essays that explore Wiesel's place in the canon of Jewish and Holocaust literature. Contains a bibliography of Wiesel's works.

Henry, Gary. "Story and Silence: Transcendence in the Work of Elie Wiesel." At http://www.elie-wiesel.com/essay.html

Although an essay posted on a website rather than printed in a peer-reviewed journal, this is an important analysis of Wiesel's work as it centers around *Night* and it is a serious consideration of Wiesel's relation to and belief regarding God in the light of the Holocaust.

Horowitz, Rosemary, ed. *Elie Wiesel and the Art of Storytelling*. Jefferson, NC: McFarland & Co., 2006.

A collection of essays concerning the influence of traditional Jewish storytelling on Wiesel's work.

Kolbert, Jack. *The Worlds of Elie Wiesel: An Overview of His Career and His Major Themes*. Selinsgrove, Penn.: Susquehanna University Press, 2001.

Kolbert discusses the principal themes that recur in Wiesel's work.

Langer, Lawrence L. *The Holocaust and the Literary Imagination*. New Haven, CT: Yale University Press, 1975.

Langer analyzes several major novels that deal with the Holocaust and includes *Night* in his study, treating it as a work of literature as well as a biographical memoir.

Rittner, Carol Ann, ed. *Elie Wiesel: Between Memory and Hope*. New York: New York University Press, 1990.

A collection of essays exploring literary and religious themes that define Wiesel's writing.

Saint-Cheron, Philippe de. *Evil and Exile*. 2nd ed. South Bend, Ind.: University of Notre Dame Press, 2000.

In a series of interviews, Wiesel and Saint-Cheron, a French journalist and archivist, discuss the problem of evil, Judeo-Christian relations, and the responsibility of bystanders in times of genocide.

Contributors

Harold Bloom is Sterling Professor of the Humanities at Yale University. He is the author of 30 books, including *Shelley's Mythmaking*, *The Visionary Company*, *Blake's Apocalypse*, *Yeats*, *A Map of Misreading*, *Kabbalah and Criticism*, *Agon: Toward a Theory of Revisionism*, *The American Religion*, *The Western Canon*, and *Omens of Millennium: The Gnosis of Angels, Dreams, and Resurrection*. *The Anxiety of Influence* sets forth Professor Bloom's provocative theory of the literary relationships between the great writers and their predecessors. His most recent books include *Shakespeare: The Invention of the Human*, a 1998 National Book Award finalist, *How to Read and Why*, *Genius: A Mosaic of One Hundred Exemplary Creative Minds*, *Hamlet: Poem Unlimited*, *Where Shall Wisdom Be Found?*, and *Jesus and Yahweh: The Names Divine*. In 1999, Professor Bloom received the prestigious American Academy of Arts and Letters Gold Medal for Criticism. He has also received the International Prize of Catalonia, the Alfonso Reyes Prize of Mexico, and the Hans Christian Andersen Bicentennial Prize of Denmark.

Alfred Kazin was an American writer, teacher, and literary critic.

Ellen S. Fine is a professor of French at Kingsborough Community College, City University of New York. She is the author of *The Absent Memory: The Act of Writing in Post-Holocaust French Literature* and *Women Writers and the Holocaust: Strategies for Survival*.

Gary Henry is a minister who works on a part-time basis with the Broadmoor Church of Christ in Nashville, Tennessee.

Peter Manseau is the author of a number of books, including *Killing the Buddha: A Heretics Bible* (with Jeff Sharlet); *Vows*, the story of his parents' marriage; and the novel *Songs for the Butcher's Daughter*.

Joseph Sungolowsky is professor of French literature and Jewish studies at Queens College. His publications include two books, *Alfred do Vigny et le dix-huitième siècle* and *Beaumarchais*, and several articles in scholarly journals such as *European Judaism* and *Midstream*.

Sabine Stein is the chief archivist at Buchenwald. Her husband, **Harry Stein**, is a researcher specializing in determining the names and biographies of persons identified in Nazi documents by numbers.

Colin Davis is a professor of history at the University of Alabama, Birmingham. He is the author of *Michel Tournier: Philosophy and Fiction* and *Levinas: An Introduction*.

Simon P. Sibelman is an associate professor of French language and literature at the University of Wisconsin-Oshkosh. He has received numerous faculty development grants as well as a research grant from the Memorial Council for Jewish Culture. He has been published in a variety of journals, including *The British Journal of Holocaust Studies* and *European Judaism*. His book-length works include *Silence in the Novels of Elie Wiesel* and *Circumscribing Swann's Nose*, a study of Jewish self-identity. He also coedited *Fractured Images*.

Ora Avni is a professor of French at Yale University. She has published extensively on nineteenth- and twentieth-century French theory and literature. She is the author of *The Resistance of Reference: Linguistics, Philosophy, and the Literary Text* and *D'un Passé l'autre: aux portes de l'histoire avec Patrick Modiano*.

Ruth Franklin is a senior editor at the *New Republic*. She is writing a book about the literature of the Holocaust.

Acknowledgments

Alfred Kazin, "The Least of These." From *The Reporter,* October 27, 1960, pp. 54–57. Copyright © 1960. Reprinted with permission of The Wylie Agency, Inc.

Ellen S. Fine, "Witness of the Night." From *Legacy of Night: The Literary Universe of Elie Wiesel.* Copyright © 1982 by SUNY Press. Reprinted with permission.

Gary Henry, "Story and Silence: Transcendence in the Work of Elie Wiesel." Reprinted with permission of the author.

Peter Manseau, "Revising Night: Elie Wiesel and the Hazards of Holocaust Theology." Reprinted with permission of the author.

Joseph Sungolowsky, "Holocaust and Autobiography: Wiesel, Friedländer, Pisar." From *Reflections on the Holocaust in Art and Literature,* edited by Randolph L. Braham, pp. 136, 138, 139–140, 140–141. Copyright © 1990. Reprinted with permission of the author.

Sabine and Harry Stein, "Buchenwald Concentration Camp, 1937–1945: Historical Survey." From *Buchenwald: A Tour of the Memorial Site.* Copyright © 1993. Reprinted with permission of the authors and the Buchenwald Memorial.

Colin Davis, "The Conversion to Ambiguity (Early Works)." From *Elie Wiesel's Secretive Texts.* Copyright © 1994 by the Board of Regents of the State of Florida. Reprinted courtesy of the University Press of Florida.

Simon P. Sibelman, "Victims to Victors: The Trilogy." From *Silence in the Novels of Elie Wiesel.* Copyright © 1995 by Simon P. Sibelman. Reprinted with permission of the author.

Index

Characters in *Night* are indexed by first name (if any).